Exceptional C++

47 Engineering Puzzles, Programming Problems, and Solutions

The C++ In-Depth Series

Bjarne Stroustrup, Editor

"I have made this letter longer than usual, because I lack the time to make it short."
—Blaise Pascal

The advent of the ISO/ANSI C++ standard marked the beginning of a new era for C++ programmers. The standard offers many new facilities and opportunities, but how can a real-world programmer find the time to discover the key nuggets of wisdom within this mass of information? **The C++ In-Depth Series** minimizes learning time and confusion by giving programmers concise, focused guides to specific topics.

Each book in this series presents a single topic, at a technical level appropriate to that topic. The Series' practical approach is designed to lift professionals to their next level of programming skills. Written by experts in the field, these short, in-depth monographs can be read and referenced without the distraction of unrelated material. The books are cross-referenced within the Series, and also reference *The C++ Programming Language* by Bjarne Stroustrup.

As you develop your skills in C++, it becomes increasingly important to separate essential information from hype and glitz, and to find the in-depth content you need in order to grow. The C++ In-Depth Series provides the tools, concepts, techniques, and new approaches to C++ that will give you a critical edge.

Titles in the Series

Accelerated C++: Practical Programming by Example, Andrew Koenig and Barbara E. Moo

Applied C++: Practical Techniques for Building Better Software, Philip Romanik and Amy Muntz

The Boost Graph Library: User Guide and Reference Manual, Jeremy G. Siek, Lie-Quan Lee, and Andrew Lumsdaine

C++ In-Depth Box Set, Bjarne Stroustrup, Andrei Alexandrescu, Andrew Koenig, Barbara E. Moo, Stanley B. Lippman, and Herb Sutter

C++ Network Programming, Volume 1: Mastering Complexity Using ACE and Patterns, Douglas C. Schmidt and Stephen D. Huston

C++ Network Programming, Volume 2: Systematic Reuse with ACE and Frameworks, Douglas C. Schmidt and Stephen D. Huston

Essential C++, Stanley B. Lippman

Exceptional C++: 47 Engineering Puzzles, Programming Problems, and Solutions, Herb Sutter

Modern C++ Design: Generic Programming and Design Patterns Applied, Andrei Alexandrescu

More Exceptional C++: 40 New Engineering Puzzles, Programming Problems, and Solutions, Herb Sutter

For more information, check out the series Web site at http://www.awprofessional.com/series/indepth/

Exceptional C++

47 Engineering Puzzles, Programming Problems, and Solutions

Herb Sutter

ADDISON–WESLEY

Boston • San Francisco • New York • Toronto • Montreal
London • Munich • Paris • Madrid
Capetown • Sydney • Tokyo • Singapore • Mexico City

The publisher offers discounts on this book when ordered in quantity for special sales. For more information, please contact:

Pearson Education Corporate Sales Division
201 W. 103rd Street
Indianapolis, IN 46290
(800) 428-5331
corpsales@pearsoned.com

Library of Congress Cataloging-in-Publication Data

Sutter, Herb.
Exceptional C++ : 47 engineering puzzles, programming problems, and solutions / Herb Sutter.
p. cm.
Includes bibliographical references and index.
ISBN 0-201-61562-2 (alk. paper)
1. C++ (Computer program language) I. Title.
QA76.73.C153.S88 1999
005.13'3—dc21 99-046115
CIP

Project Editor: Deborah Lafferty
Production Manager: Sarah Weaver
Design and Composition: Kim Arney
Index: Michael Loo

Text printed on recycled and acid-free paper.

ISBN 0201615622

8 9 10111213 CRS 06 05 04 03

8th Printing May 2003

To my family for their patient support,
and to Eric Wilson, Jeff Sumner, Juana Chang, Larry Palmer,
and the rest of the core PeerDirect development team,
my "extended family" for the past four years:

Declan West
Doug Shelley
Duk Loi
Ian Long
Justin Karabegovic
Kim Nguyen
Margot Fulcher
Mark Cheers
Morgan Jones
Violetta Lukow

Thanks for everything, guys.

Contents

Foreword

This is a remarkable book, but it wasn't until I had nearly finished reading it that I realized just how remarkable it is. This could well be the first book ever written for people who are already familiar with C++—*all* of C++. From language features to components of the standard library to programming techniques, this book skips from topic to topic, always keeping you slightly off balance, always making sure you're paying attention. Just like real C++ programs. Class design bumps into the behavior of virtual functions, iterator conventions run up against name lookup rules, assignment operators sideswipe exception safety, compilation dependencies cross paths with exported templates. Just like they do in real programs. The result is a dizzying maelstrom of language features, library components, and programming techniques at once both chaotic and magnificent. Just like real programs.

I pronounce *GotW* such that it rhymes with "Gotcha," and perhaps that's fitting. As I compared my solutions to the book's quizzes against Sutter's answers, I fell into the traps he (and C++) laid before me more often than I'd like to admit. I could almost see Herb smiling and softly saying "Gotcha!" for each error I made. Some may argue that this proves I don't know much about C++. Others may claim it demonstrates that C++ is too complex for anyone to master. I believe it shows that when you're working in C++, you have to think carefully about what you're doing. C++ is a powerful language designed to help solve demanding problems, and it's important that you hone your knowledge of the language, its library, and its programming idioms as finely as you can. The breadth of topics in this book will help you do that. So will its unique quiz-based format.

Veteran readers of the C++ newsgroups know how difficult it is to be proclaimed a *Guru of the Week*. Veteran participants know it even better. On the Internet, of course, there can be only one guru each week, but, backed by the information in this book, you can reasonably hope to produce guru-quality code every time you program.

Scott Meyers
June 1999

Preface

Exceptional C++ shows by example how to go about solid software engineering. Along with a lot of other material, this book includes expanded versions of the first 30 issues of the popular Internet C++ feature *Guru of the Week* (or, in its short form, *GotW*), a series of self-contained C++ engineering problems and solutions that illustrate specific design and coding techniques.

This book isn't a random grab-bag of code puzzles; it's primarily a guide to sound real-world enterprise software design in C++. It uses a problem/solution format because that's the most effective way I know to involve you, gentle reader, in the ideas behind the problems and the reasons behind the guidelines. Although the Items cover a variety of topics, you'll notice recurring themes that focus on enterprise development issues, particularly exception safety, sound class and module design, appropriate optimization, and writing portable standards-conforming code.

I hope you find this material useful in your daily work. But I also hope you find at least a few nifty thoughts and elegant techniques, and that from time to time, as you're reading through these pages, you'll suddenly have an "Aha! Gnarly!" moment. After all, who says software engineering has to be dull?

How to Read This Book

I expect that you already know the basics of C++. If you don't, start with a good C++ introduction and overview (good choices are a classic tome like Bjarne Stroustrup's *The C++ Programming Language, Third Edition*[1] or Stan Lippman and Josée Lajoie's *C++ Primer, Third Edition*[2]), and then be sure to pick up a style guide like Scott Meyers' classic *Effective C++* books (I find the browser-based CD version convenient and useful).[3]

1. Stroustrup B. *The C++ Programming Language, Third Edition* (Addison Wesley Longman, 1997).
2. Lippman S. and Lajoie J. *C++ Primer, Third Edition* (Addison Wesley Longman, 1998).
3. Meyers S. *Effective C++ CD: 85 Specific Ways to Improve Your Programs and Designs* (Addison Wesley Longman, 1999). An online demo is available at http://www.meyerscd.awl.com.

Each item in this book is presented as a puzzle or problem, with an introductory header that looks like this:

ITEM ##: THE TOPIC OF THIS PUZZLE **DIFFICULTY: X**

The topic tag and difficulty rating (typically anything from 3 to 9½, based on a scale of 10) gives you a hint of what you're in for. Note that the difficulty rating is my own subjective guess at how difficult I expect most people will find each problem, so you may well find that a given 7 problem is easier for you than another 5 problem. Still, it's better to be prepared for the worst when you see a 9½ monster coming down the pike.

You don't have to read the sections and problems in order, but in several places there are "miniseries" of related problems that you'll see designated as "Part 1," "Part 2," and so on—some all the way up to "Part 10." Those miniseries are best read as a group.

This book includes many guidelines, in which the following words usually carry a specific meaning:

- **always** = This is absolutely necessary. Never fail to do this.
- **prefer** = This is usually the right way. Do it another way only when a situation specifically warrants it.
- **consider** = This may or may not apply, but it's something to think about.
- **avoid** = This is usually not the best way, and might even be dangerous. Look for alternatives, and do it this way only when a situation specifically warrants it.
- **never** = This is extremely bad. Don't even think about it. Career limiting move.

Finally, a word about URLs: On the Web, stuff moves. In particular, stuff I have no control over moves. That makes it a real pain to publish random Web URLs in a print book lest they become out of date before the book makes it to the printer's, never mind after it's been sitting on your desk for five years. When I reference other people's articles or Web sites in this book, I do it via a URL on my own Web site, www.gotw.ca, which I can control and which contains just a straight redirect to the real Web page. If you find that a link printed in this book no longer works, send me e-mail and tell me; I'll update that redirector to point to the new page's location (if I can find the page again) or to say that the page no longer exists (if I can't). Either way, this book's URLs will stay up to date despite the rigors of print media in an Internet world. Whew.

---

3. Meyers S. *Effective C++ CD: 85 Specific Ways to Improve Your Programs and Designs* (Addison Wesley Longman, 1999). An online demo is available at http://www.meyerscd.awl.com.

How We Got Here: *GotW* and PeerDirect

The C++ *Guru of the Week* series has come a long way. *GotW* was originally created late in 1996 to provide interesting challenges and ongoing education for our own development team here at PeerDirect. I wrote it to provide an entertaining learning tool, including rants on things like the proper use of inheritance and exception safety. As time went on, I also used it as a means to provide our team with visibility to the changes being made at the C++ standards meetings. Since then, *GotW* has been made available to the general C++ public as a regular feature of the Internet newsgroup *comp.lang.c++.moderated*, where you can find each new issue's questions and answers (and a lot of interesting discussion).

Using C++ well is important at PeerDirect for many of the same reasons it's important in your company, if perhaps to achieve different goals. We happen to build systems software—for distributed databases and database replication—in which enterprise issues such as reliability, safety, portability, efficiency, and many others are make-or-break concerns. The software we write needs to be able to be ported across various compilers and operating systems; it needs to be safe and robust in the presence of database transaction deadlocks and communications interruptions and programming exceptions; and it's used by customers to manage tiny databases sitting inside smart cards and pop machines or on PalmOS and WinCE devices, through to departmental Windows NT and Linux and Solaris servers, through to massively parallel Oracle back-ends for Web servers and data warehouses—with the same software, the same reliability, the same code. Now *that's* a portability and reliability challenge, as we creep up on half a million tight, noncomment lines of code.

To those of you who have been reading *Guru of the Week* on the Internet for the past few years, I have a couple of things to say:

- Thank you for your interest, support, e-mails, kudos, corrections, comments, criticisms, questions—and especially for your requests for the *GotW* series to be assembled in book form. Here it is; I hope you enjoy it.
- This book contains *a lot* more than you ever saw on the Internet.

Exceptional C++ is not just a cut-and-paste of stale *GotW* issues that are already floating out there somewhere in cyberspace. All the problems and solutions have been considerably revised and reworked—for example, Items 8 through 17 on exception safety originally appeared as a single *GotW* puzzle and have now become an in-depth, 10-part miniseries. Each problem and solution has been examined to bring it up to date with the then-changing, and now official, C++ standard.

So, if you've been a regular reader of *GotW* before, there's a lot that's new here for you. To all faithful readers, thanks again, and I hope this material will help you continue to hone and expand your software engineering and C++ programming skills.

Acknowledgments

First, of course, thanks to all the *GotW* readers and enthusiasts on *comp.lang.c++.moderated*, especially the scores of people who participated in the contest to select a name for this book. Two in particular were instrumental in leading us to the final title, and I want to thank them specifically: Marco Dalla Gasperina for suggesting the name *Enlightened C++*, and Rob Stewart for suggesting the name *Practical C++ Problems and Solutions*. It was only natural to take these a step further and insert the pun *exceptional,* given the repeated emphasis herein on exception safety.

Many thanks also to series editor Bjarne Stroustrup and to Marina Lang, Debbie Lafferty, and the rest of the Addison Wesley Longman editorial staff for their continued interest and enthusiasm in this project, and for hosting a really nice reception at the Santa Cruz C++ standards meeting in 1998.

I also want to thank the many people who acted as reviewers—many of them fellow standards-committee members—who provided thoughtful and incisive comments that have helped to improve the text you are about to read. Special thanks to Bjarne Stroustrup and Scott Meyers, and to Andrei Alexandrescu, Steve Clamage, Steve Dewhurst, Cay Horstmann, Jim Hyslop, Brendan Kehoe, and Dennis Mancl, for their invaluable insights and reviews.

Finally, thanks most of all to my family and friends for always being there, in so many different ways.

Herb Sutter
June 1999

Generic Programming and the C++ Standard Library

To begin, let's consider a few selected topics in the area of generic programming. These puzzles focus on the effective use of templates, iterators, and algorithms, and how to use and extend standard library facilities. These ideas then lead nicely into the following section, which analyzes exception safety in the context of writing exception-safe templates.

Item 1: Iterators — Difficulty: 7

Every programmer who uses the standard library has to be aware of these common and not-so-common iterator mistakes. How many of them can you find?

The following program has at least four iterator-related problems. How many can you find?

```
int main()
{
  vector<Date> e;
  copy( istream_iterator<Date>( cin ),
        istream_iterator<Date>(),
        back_inserter( e ) );
  vector<Date>::iterator first =
        find( e.begin(), e.end(), "01/01/95" );
  vector<Date>::iterator last =
        find( e.begin(), e.end(), "12/31/95" );
  *last = "12/30/95";
  copy( first,
        last,
        ostream_iterator<Date>( cout, "\n" ) );
  e.insert( --e.end(), TodaysDate() );
  copy( first,
        last,
        ostream_iterator<Date>( cout, "\n" ) );
}
```

Solution

```
int main()
{
  vector<Date> e;
  copy( istream_iterator<Date>( cin ),
        istream_iterator<Date>(),
        back_inserter( e ) );
```

This is fine so far. The `Date` class writer provided an extractor function with the signature `operator>>( istream&, Date& )`, which is what `istream_iterator<Date>` uses to read the `Dates` from the `cin` stream. The `copy()` algorithm just stuffs the `Dates` into the vector.

```
  vector<Date>::iterator first =
        find( e.begin(), e.end(), "01/01/95" );
  vector<Date>::iterator last =
        find( e.begin(), e.end(), "12/31/95" );
  *last = "12/30/95";
```

Error: This may be illegal, because `last` may be `e.end()` and therefore not a dereferenceable iterator.

The `find()` algorithm returns its second argument (the end iterator of the range) if the value is not found. In this case, if "12/31/95" is not in `e`, then `last` is equal to `e.end()`, which points to one-past-the-end of the container and is not a valid iterator.

```
  copy( first,
        last,
        ostream_iterator<Date>( cout, "\n" ) );
```

Error: This may be illegal because `[first,last)` may not be a valid range; indeed, `first` may actually be after `last`.

For example, if "01/01/95" is not found in `e` but "12/31/95" is, then the iterator `last` will point to something earlier in the collection (the `Date` object equal to "12/31/95") than does the iterator `first` (one past the end). However, `copy()` requires that `first` must point to an earlier place in the same collection as `last`—that is, `[first,last)` must be a valid range.

Unless you're using a checked version of the standard library that can detect some of these problems for you, the likely symptom if this happens will be a difficult-to-diagnose core dump during or sometime after the `copy()`.

```
  e.insert( --e.end() , TodaysDate() );
```

First error: The expression "`--e.end()`" is likely to be illegal.

The reason is simple, if a little obscure: On popular implementations of the standard library, `vector<Date>::iterator` is often simply a `Date*`, and the C++ language doesn't allow you to modify temporaries of builtin type. For example, the following plain-jane code is also illegal:

```
Date* f();      // function that returns a Date*
p = --f();      // error, but could be "f() - 1"
```

Fortunately, we know that `vector<Date>::iterator` is a random-access iterator, so there's no loss of efficiency in writing this (more) correctly as:

```
e.insert( e.end() - 1, TodaysDate() );
```

Second error: Now you still have the other error, which is: If `e` is empty, any attempt to take "the iterator before `e.end()`" (whether you spell that "`--e.end()`" or "`e.end()-1`") will not be a valid iterator.

```
    copy( first,
          last,
          ostream_iterator<Date>( cout, "\n" ) );
}
```

Error: `first` and `last` may not be valid iterators any more.

A `vector` grows in "chunks" so that it won't have to reallocate its buffer every time you insert something into it. However, sometimes the `vector` will be full, and adding something will trigger a reallocation.

Here, as a result of the `e.insert()` operation, the vector may or may not grow, which means its memory may or may not move. Because of this uncertainty, we must consider any existing iterators into that container to be invalidated. In this case, if the memory really did move, then the buggy `copy()` will again generally manifest as a difficult-to-diagnose core dump.

Guideline

Never dereference an invalid iterator.

To summarize: When using iterators, be aware of four main issues.

1. Valid values: Is the iterator dereferenceable? For example, writing "`*e.end()`" is always a programming error.
2. Valid lifetimes: Is the iterator still valid when it's being used? Or has it been invalidated by some operation since we obtained it?
3. Valid ranges: Is a pair of iterators a valid range? Is `first` really before (or equal to) `last`? Do both really point into the same container?
4. Illegal builtin manipulation: For example, is the code trying to modify a temporary of builtin type, as in "`--e.end()`" above? (Fortunately, the compiler can often catch this kind of mistake for you, and for iterators of class type, the library author will often choose to allow this sort of thing for syntactic convenience.)

Item 2: Case-Insensitive Strings—Part 1 Difficulty: 7

So you want a case-insensitive string class? Your mission, should you choose to accept it, is to write one.

This Item is composed of three related points.

1. What does "*case-insensitive*" mean?
2. Write a `ci_string` class that is identical to the standard `std::string` class but that is case-insensitive in the same way as the commonly provided extension `stricmp()`.[1] A `ci_string` should be usable as follows:

```
ci_string s( "AbCdE" );
// case insensitive
//
assert( s == "abcde" );
assert( s == "ABCDE" );
// still case-preserving, of course
//
assert( strcmp( s.c_str(), "AbCdE" ) == 0 );
assert( strcmp( s.c_str(), "abcde" ) != 0 );
```

3. Is making case sensitivity a property of the object a good idea?

Solution

The answers to the three questions are as follows.

1. What does "*case-insensitive*" mean?

What "*case-insensitive*" actually means depends entirely on your application and language. For example, many languages do not have cases at all. For those that do, you still have to decide whether you want accented characters to compare equal to unaccented characters, and so on. This Item provides guidance on how to implement case-insensitivity for standard strings in whatever sense applies to your situation.

2. Write a `ci_string` class that is identical to the standard `std::string` class but that is case-insensitive in the same way as the commonly provided extension `stricmp()`.

The "how can I make a case-insensitive string?" question is so common that it probably deserves its own FAQ—hence this Item.

1. The `stricmp()` case-insensitive string comparison function is not part of the C or C++ standards, but it is a common extension on many C and C++ compilers.

Here's what we want to achieve:

```
ci_string s( "AbCdE" );
// case insensitive
//
assert( s == "abcde" );
assert( s == "ABCDE" );
// still case-preserving, of course
//
assert( strcmp( s.c_str(), "AbCdE" ) == 0 );
assert( strcmp( s.c_str(), "abcde" ) != 0 );
```

The key here is to understand what a `string` actually is in Standard C++. If you look in your trusty `string` header, you'll see something like this:

```
typedef basic_string<char> string;
```

So `string` isn't really a class; it's a `typedef` of a template. In turn, the `basic_string<>` template is declared as follows, possibly with additional implementation-specific template parameters:

```
template<class charT,
         class traits = char_traits<charT>,
         class Allocator = allocator<charT> >
class basic_string;
```

So "`string`" really means "`basic_string<char, char_traits<char>, allocator<char> >`," possibly with additional defaulted template parameters specific to the implementation you're using. We don't need to worry about the `allocator` part, but the key here is the `char_traits` part, because `char_traits` defines how characters interact—and compare!

So let's compare `string`s. `basic_string` supplies useful comparison functions that let you compare whether one `string` is equal to another, less than another, and so on. These `string` comparison functions are built on top of character comparison functions supplied in the `char_traits` template. In particular, the `char_traits` template supplies character comparison functions named `eq()` and `lt()` for equality and less-than comparisons, and `compare()` and `find()` functions to compare and search sequences of characters.

If we want these to behave differently, all we have to do is provide a different `char_traits` template. Here's the easiest way:

```
struct ci_char_traits : public char_traits<char>
              // just inherit all the other functions
              //  that we don't need to replace
{
  static bool eq( char c1, char c2 )
    { return toupper(c1) == toupper(c2); }
  static bool lt( char c1, char c2 )
    { return toupper(c1) <  toupper(c2); }
  static int compare( const char* s1,
                      const char* s2,
                      size_t n )
```

```
    { return memicmp( s1, s2, n ); }
            // if available on your platform,
            //  otherwise you can roll your own
  static const char*
  find( const char* s, int n, char a )
  {
    while( n-- > 0 && toupper(*s) != toupper(a) )
    {
        ++s;
    }
    return n >= 0 ? s : 0;
  }
};
```

And finally, the key that brings it all together:

```
typedef basic_string<char, ci_char_traits> ci_string;
```

All we've done is create a `typedef` named `ci_string` that operates exactly like the standard `string` (after all, in most respects it *is* the standard `string`), except that it uses `ci_char_traits` instead of `char_traits<char>` to get its character comparison rules. Since we've handily made the `ci_char_traits` rules case-insensitive, we've made `ci_string` itself case-insensitive, without any further surgery—that is, we have a case-insensitive string without having touched `basic_string` at all. Now *that's* extensibility.

3. Is making the case sensitivity a property of the object a good idea?

It's often more useful to have case sensitivity be a property of the comparison function instead of a property of the object as shown here. For example, consider the following code:

```
string    a = "aaa";
ci_string b = "aAa";
if( a == b ) /* ... */
```

Given a suitable `operator==()`, should the expression "`a == b`" evaluate to `true`, or to `false`? We could easily take the view that if either side were case-insensitive, the comparison should be case-insensitive. But what if we change the example just a little and introduce yet another instantiation of `basic_string` that does comparisons a third way:

```
typedef basic_string<char, yz_char_traits> yz_string;

ci_string b = "aAa";
yz_string c = "AAa";
if( b == c ) /* ... */
```

Now, consider the question again: Should the expression "`a == b`" evaluate to `true` or to `false`? In this case, I think you'll agree that it's less obvious that we should arbitrarily prefer one object's ordering over another's.

Instead, consider how much clearer the examples would be when written as follows:

```
string a = "aaa";
string b = "aAa";
if( stricmp( a.c_str(), b.c_str() ) == 0 ) /* ... */
string c = "AAa";
if( EqualUsingYZComparison( b, c ) ) /* ... */
```

In many cases, it's more useful to have the case sensitivity be a characteristic of the comparison operation. But I've encountered cases in practice in which making it a characteristic of the object (especially when most or all comparisons were with C-style `char*` strings) is much more useful because you can simply compare values "naturally" (i.e., "`if ( a == "text" ) ...`") without having to remember to use the case-insensitive comparison every time.

This Item should give you a flavor for how the `basic_string` template works and how flexible it is in practice. If you want different comparisons than the ones `memicmp()` and `toupper()` provide, just replace the five functions shown here with your own code that performs character comparisons that are appropriate to your application.

Item 3: Case-Insensitive Strings—Part 2 — Difficulty: 5

How usable is the `ci_string` we created in Item 2? Now we'll focus on usability issues, see what design problems or tradeoffs we encounter, and fill in some of the remaining gaps.

Consider again the solution for Item 2 (ignoring the function bodies):

```
struct ci_char_traits : public char_traits<char>
{
  static bool eq( char c1, char c2 )   { /*...*/ }
  static bool lt( char c1, char c2 )   { /*...*/ }
  static int compare( const char* s1,
                      const char* s2,
                      size_t n )       { /*...*/ }
  static const char*
  find( const char* s, int n, char a ) { /*...*/ }
};
```

For this Item, answer the following related questions as completely as possible:

1. Is it safe to inherit `ci_char_traits` from `char_traits<char>` this way?
2. Why does the following code fail to compile?

```
ci_string s = "abc";
cout << s << endl;
```

3. What about using other operators (for example, +, +=, =) and mixing strings and ci_strings as arguments? For example:

```
string    a = "aaa";
ci_string b = "bbb";
string    c = a + b;
```

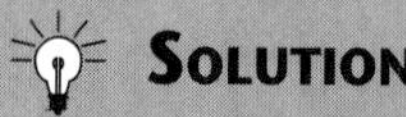

Solution

The answers to the three questions are as follows.

1. Is it safe to inherit ci_char_traits from char_traits<char> this way?

Public inheritance should normally model IS-A / WORKS-LIKE-A as per the Liskov Substitution Principle (LSP). (See Items 22 and 28.) This, however, is one of the rare exceptions to the LSP, because ci_char_traits is not intended to be used polymorphically through a pointer or reference to the base class char_traits<char>. The standard library does not use traits objects polymorphically. In this case, inheritance is used merely for convenience (well, some would say laziness); inheritance is not being used in an object-oriented way.

On the other hand, the LSP does still apply in another sense: It applies at compile-time, when the derived object must WORK-LIKE-A base object in the ways required by the basic_string template's requirements. In a newsgroup posting, Nathan Myers[2] puts it this way:

> *In other words, LSP applies, but only at compile-time, and by the convention we call "requirements lists." I would like to distinguish this case; call it Generic Liskov Substitution Principle (GLSP): Any type (or template) passed as a template argument should conform to the requirements listed for that argument.*
>
> *Classes derived from iterator tags and traits classes, then, are subject to GLSP, but classical LSP considerations (for example, virtual destructor, and so forth) may or may not apply, depending on whether run-time polymorphic behaviors are in the signature specified in the requirements list.*

So, in short, this inheritance is safe, because it conforms to GLSP (if not LSP). However, the main reason I used it here was not for convenience (to avoid writing all the other char_traits<char> baggage), but to demonstrate *what's different*—that we had to change only four operations to get the effect we want.

The reason behind this first question was to get you to think about several things: (1) the proper uses (and improper abuses) of inheritance; (2) the implications of the fact that there are only static members; (3) the fact that char_traits objects are never used polymorphically.

2. Nathan is a longtime member of the C++ standards committee and the primary author of the standard's locale facility.

2. Why does the following code fail to compile?

```
ci_string s = "abc";
cout << s << endl;
```

Hint: From 21.3.7.9 [lib.string.io] in the C++ standard, the declaration of operator<< for basic_string is specified as:

```
template<class charT, class traits, class Allocator>
basic_ostream<charT, traits>&
operator<<(basic_ostream<charT, traits>& os,
           const basic_string<charT,traits,Allocator>& str);
```

Answer: Notice first that cout is actually a basic_ostream<char, char_traits<char> >. Then we can spot the problem: operator<< for basic_string is templated and all, but it's specified only for insertion into a basic_ostream with the same "char type" and "traits type" as the string. That is, the standard operator<< will let you output a ci_string to a basic_ostream<char, ci_char_traits>, which isn't what cout is, even though ci_char_traits inherits from char_traits<char> in the above solution.

There are two ways to resolve this: Define operator<<() and operator>>() for ci_strings yourself, or tack on ".c_str()" to use operator<<(const char*) if your application's strings don't have embedded nulls:

```
cout << s.c_str() << endl;
```

3. What about using other operators (for example, +, +=, =) and mixing strings and ci_strings as arguments? For example:

```
string    a = "aaa";
ci_string b = "bbb";
string    c = a + b;
```

Again, there are two ways to deal with this: Either define your own operator+() functions, or tack on ".c_str()" to use operator+(const char*):

```
string    c = a + b.c_str();
```

Item 4: Maximally Reusable Generic Containers—Part 1 — Difficulty: 8

How flexible can you make this simple container class? Hint: You'll learn more than a little about member templates along the way.

How can you best implement copy construction and copy assignment for the following fixed-length vector class? How can you provide maximum usability for construction and assignment? Hint: Think about the kinds of things that client code might want to do.

```
template<typename T, size_t size>
class fixed_vector
{
public:
  typedef T*       iterator;
  typedef const T* const_iterator;
  iterator       begin()       { return v_; }
  iterator       end()         { return v_+size; }
  const_iterator begin() const { return v_; }
  const_iterator end()   const { return v_+size; }

private:
  T v_[size];
};
```

Note: Don't fix other things. This container is not intended to be fully STL-compliant, and it has at least one subtle problem. It's meant only to illustrate some important issues in a simplified setting.

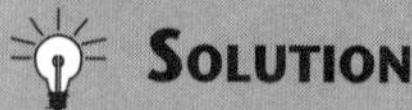

Solution

For this Item's solution, we'll do something a little different. I'll present a proposed solution, and your mission is to supply the explanation and critique the solution. Consider now Item 5.

Item 5: Maximally Reusable Generic Containers—Part 2 — Difficulty: 6

Historical note: The example used in this Item is adapted from one presented by Kevlin Henney and later analyzed by Jon Jagger in issues 12 and 20 of the British C++ magazine Overload. *(British readers beware: The answer to this Item goes well beyond that presented in* Overload *#20. In fact, the efficiency optimization presented there won't work in the solution to this problem.)*

What is the following solution doing, and why? Explain each constructor and operator. Does this design or code have any flaws?

```
template<typename T, size_t size>
class fixed_vector
{
```

```
public:
  typedef T*       iterator;
  typedef const T* const_iterator;
  fixed_vector() { }

  template<typename O, size_t osize>
  fixed_vector( const fixed_vector<O,osize>& other )
  {
    copy( other.begin(),
          other.begin()+min(size,osize),
          begin() );
  }

  template<typename O, size_t osize>
  fixed_vector<T,size>&
  operator=( const fixed_vector<O,osize>& other )
  {
    copy( other.begin(),
          other.begin()+min(size,osize),
          begin() );
    return *this;
  }

  iterator       begin()       { return v_; }
  iterator       end()         { return v_+size; }
  const_iterator begin() const { return v_; }
  const_iterator end()   const { return v_+size; }

private:
  T v_[size];
};
```

Solution

Let's analyze the solution above and see how well it measures up to what the question asked. Recall that the original question was: How can you best implement copy construction and copy assignment for the following fixed-length vector class? How can you provide maximum usability for construction and assignment? Hint: Think about the kinds of things that client code might want to do.

Copy Construction and Copy Assignment

First, note that the first question is a red herring. Did you spot it? The original code already had a copy constructor and a copy assignment operator that worked just fine, thank you very much. Our solution proposes to address the second question by adding a templated constructor and a templated assignment operator to make construction and assignment more flexible.

```
template<typename O, size_t osize>
fixed_vector( const fixed_vector<O,osize>& other )
{
  copy( other.begin(),
        other.begin()+min(size,osize),
        begin() );
}

template<typename O, size_t osize>
fixed_vector<T,size>&
operator=( const fixed_vector<O,osize>& other )
{
  copy( other.begin(),
        other.begin()+min(size,osize),
        begin() );
  return *this;
}
```

Note that the above functions are *not* a copy constructor and a copy assignment operator. Here's why: A copy constructor or copy assignment operator specifically constructs/assigns from another object of exactly the same type—including the same template arguments, if the class is templated. For example:

```
struct X
{
  template<typename T>
  X( const T& );    // NOT copy constructor, T can't be X

  template<typename T>
  operator=( const T& );
                    // NOT copy assignment, T can't be X
};
```

"But," you say, "those two templated member functions could exactly match the signatures of copy construction and copy assignment!" Well, actually, no—they couldn't, because in both cases, `T` may not be `X`. To quote from the standard (12.8/2, note 4):

> *Because* a template constructor is never a copy constructor, *the presence of such a template does not suppress the implicit declaration of a copy constructor. Template constructors participate in overload resolution with other constructors, including copy constructors, and a template constructor may be used to copy an object if it provides a better match than other constructors.*

There's similar wording for the copy assignment operator (in 12.8/9 note 7). So the proposed solution, in fact, still has the same copy constructor and copy assignment operator as the original code, because the compiler still generates the implicit versions. What we've done is extend the construction and assignment flexibility, not replace the old versions.

For another example, consider the following program:

```
fixed_vector<char,4> v;
fixed_vector<int,4>  w;
fixed_vector<int,4>  w2(w);
        // calls implicit copy constructor
fixed_vector<int,4>  w3(v);
        // calls templated conversion constructor
w = w2; // calls implicit copy assignment operator
w = v;  // calls templated assignment operator
```

So the question really wanted us to provide flexible "construction and assignment from other `fixed_vector`s," not specifically flexible "copy construction and copy assignment," which already existed.

Usability Issues for Construction and Assignment

There are two major usability considerations.

1. Support varying types (including inheritance).

While `fixed_vector` definitely is and should remain a homogeneous container, sometimes it makes sense to construct or assign from another `fixed_vector` that actually contains different objects. As long as the source objects are assignable to our type of object, this should be allowed. For example, clients may want to write something like this:

```
fixed_vector<char,4> v;
fixed_vector<int,4>  w(v);  // templated construction
w = v;                      // templated assignment

class B           { /*...*/ };
class D : public B { /*...*/ };

fixed_vector<D*,4> x;
fixed_vector<B*,4> y(x);    // templated construction
y = x;                      // templated assignment
```

This is legal and works as expected because a `D*` can be assigned to a `B*`.

2. Support varying sizes.

Similarly, clients may want to construct or assign from `fixed_vector`s with different sizes. Again, it makes sense to support this feature. For example:

```
fixed_vector<char,6> v;
fixed_vector<int,4>  w(v);  // initializes using 4 values
w = v;                      // assigns using 4 values
class B           { /*...*/ };
class D : public B { /*...*/ };
fixed_vector<D*,16> x;
fixed_vector<B*,42> y(x);   // initializes using 16 values
y = x;                      // assigns using 16 values
```

Alternative: The Standard Library Approach

I happen to like the syntax and usability of the preceding functions, but there are still some nifty things they won't let you do. Consider another approach that follows the style of the standard library.

1. Copying

```
template<class RAIter>
fixed_vector( RAIter first, RAIter last )
{
  copy( first,
        first+min(size,(size_t)last-first),
        begin() );
}
```

Now when copying, instead of writing:

```
fixed_vector<char,6> v;
fixed_vector<int,4>  w(v);  // initialize using 4 values
```

we need to write:

```
fixed_vector<char,6> v;
fixed_vector<int,4>  w(v.begin(), v.end());
                            // initialize using 4 values
```

Stop and think about this for a moment. What do you think of it? For construction, which style is better—the style of our proposed solution or this standard library-like style?

In this case, our initial proposed solution is somewhat easier to use, whereas the standard library-like style is much more flexible (for example, it allows users to choose subranges and copy from other kinds of containers). You can take your pick or simply supply both flavors.

2. Assignment

Note that we can't templatize assignment to take an iterator range, because `operator=()` may take only one parameter. Instead, we can provide a named function:

```
template<class Iter>
fixed_vector<T,size>&
assign( Iter first, Iter last )
{
  copy( first,
        first+min(size,(size_t)last-first),
        begin() );
  return *this;
}
```

Now when assigning, instead of writing:

```
w = v;                      // assign using 4 values
```

we need to write:

```
w.assign(v.begin(), v.end());
                              // assign using 4 value
```

Technically, assign() isn't even necessary, because we could still get the same flexibility without it, but that would be uglier and less efficient:

```
w = fixed_vector<int,4>(v.begin(), v.end());
    // initialize and assign using 4 values
```

Again, stop and consider these alternatives. For assignment, which style is better—the style of our proposed solution or this standard library-like style?

This time, the flexibility argument doesn't hold water because the user can just as easily (and even more flexibly) write the copy himself. Instead of writing:

```
w.assign( v.begin(), v.end() );
```

the user just writes:

```
copy( v.begin(), v.begin()+4, w.begin() );
```

So there's little reason to write an iterator-range assign() in this case. And for assignment, it's probably best to use the technique from the proposed solution and let clients use copy() directly whenever subrange assignment is desired.

Why Write the Default Constructor?

Finally, why does the proposed solution also write an empty default constructor, which merely does the same thing as the compiler-generated default constructor?

The answer is short and sweet: This is necessary because as soon as you define a constructor of any kind, the compiler will not generate the default one for you, and, clearly, client code such as the above requires it.

A Lingering Problem

This Item's question also asked: Does this design or code have any flaws?

Perhaps. Later in this book we'll distinguish between various exception safety guarantees (see Items 8 to 11, and page 38). Like the compiler-generated copy assignment operator, our templated assignment operator provides the basic guarantee, which can be perfectly fine. Just for a moment, though, let's explore what happens if we do want it to provide the strong guarantee, to make it *strongly* exception-safe. Recall that the templated assignment operator was defined as:

```
template<typename O, size_t osize>
fixed_vector<T,size>&
operator=( const fixed_vector<O,osize>& other )
{
```

```
    copy( other.begin(),
          other.begin()+min(size,osize),
          begin() );
    return *this;
  }
```

If one of the T assignments fails during the copy() operation, the object will be in an inconsistent state. Some of the contents of our fixed_vector object will be what they were before the failed assignment, but other parts of the contents will already have been updated.

Alas, as it is currently designed, fixed_vector *cannot be made strongly exception-safe for assignment*. Why not? Because of the following:

- Normally, the right (and easiest) way to solve this is to supply an atomic and nonthrowing Swap() function that swaps the guts of two fixed_vector objects, and then simply use the canonical (and, this time, templated) form of operator=(), which simply uses the create-a-temporary-and-swap idiom. See Item 13 for details.
- There's no way to write an atomic nonthrowing Swap() that exchanges the internals of two fixed_vector objects. This is because the fixed_vector internals are stored as a simple array that can't be copied in one atomic step—which, after all, was the very problem with our proposed operator=() that got us onto this side track.

But don't despair just yet. There is, indeed, a good solution, but it involves changing fixed_vector's design—if only ever so slightly—so that it stores its contents as a dynamically allocated array instead of as a member array. True, this eliminates the efficiency advantage of fixed_vector, and it means we have to write a destructor—but such can be the price of strong exception safety.

```
// A strongly exception-safe version:
//
template<typename T, size_t size>
class fixed_vector
{
public:
  typedef T*       iterator;
  typedef const T* const_iterator;

  fixed_vector() : v_( new T[size] ) { }

  ~fixed_vector() { delete[] v_; }

  template<typename O, size_t osize>
  fixed_vector( const fixed_vector<O,osize>& other )
    : v_( new T[size] )
    { try {copy(other.begin(),other.begin()+min(size,osize),
                begin());}
      catch(...) { delete[] v_; throw; } }
```

```
    fixed_vector( const fixed_vector<T,size>& other )
      : v_( new T[size] )
      { try {copy(other.begin(), other.end(), begin());}
        catch(...) { delete[] v_; throw; } }

    void Swap( fixed_vector<T,size>& other ) throw()
    {
      swap( v_, other.v_ );
    }

    template<typename O, size_t osize>
    fixed_vector<T,size>& operator=(
      const fixed_vector<O,osize>& other )
    {
      fixed_vector<T,size> temp( other ); // does all the work
      Swap( temp ); return *this;         // this can't throw
    }
    fixed_vector<T,size>& operator=(
      const fixed_vector<T,size>& other ) {
      fixed_vector<T,size> temp( other ); // does all the work
      Swap( temp ); return *this;         // this can't throw
    }

    iterator       begin()       { return v_; }
    iterator       end()         { return v_+size; }
    const_iterator begin() const { return v_; }
    const_iterator end()   const { return v_+size; }

  private:
    T* v_;
  };
```

Common Mistake

Never make exception safety an afterthought. Exception safety affects a class's design. It is never "just an implementation detail."

To summarize: This Item, I hope, has convinced you that member function templates are handy. I hope it's also helped to show why they're widely used in the standard library. If you're not familiar with them already, don't despair. Not all compilers support member templates today, but they're in the standard, therefore all compilers will soon.

Use member templates to good effect when creating your own classes and you'll likely not just have happy users, but more of them, as they flock to reuse the code that's best designed for reuse.

Item 6: Temporary Objects — Difficulty: 5

Unnecessary and/or temporary objects are frequent culprits that can throw all your hard work—and your program's performance—right out the window. How can you spot them and avoid them?

("Temporary objects?" you might be wondering. "That's more of an optimization thing. What's that got to do with generic programming and the standard library?" Bear with me; the reason will become clear in the following Item.)

You are doing a code review. A programmer has written the following function, which uses unnecessary temporary objects in at least three places. How many can you identify, and how should the programmer fix them?

```
string FindAddr( list<Employee> emps, string name )
{
  for( list<Employee>::iterator i = emps.begin();
       i != emps.end();
       i++ )
  {
    if( *i == name )
    {
      return i->addr;
    }
  }
  return "";
}
```

Do not change the operational semantics of this function, even though they could be improved.

Solution

Believe it or not, this short function harbors three obvious cases of unnecessary temporaries, two subtler ones, and two red herrings.

The two more-obvious temporaries are buried in the function declaration itself:

```
string FindAddr( list<Employee> emps, string name )
```

The parameters should be passed by `const&`—that is, `const list<Employee>&` and `const string&`, respectively—instead of by value. Pass-by-value forces the compiler to make complete copies of both objects, which can be expensive and, here, is completely unnecessary.

Guideline

Prefer passing objects by `const&` *instead of passing by value.*

The third more-obvious avoidable temporary occurs in the `for` loop's termination condition:

```
for( /*...*/ ; i != emps.end() ; /*...*/ )
```

For most containers (including list), calling `end()` returns a temporary object that must be constructed and destroyed. Because the value will not change, recomputing (and reconstructing and redestroying) it on every loop iteration is both needlessly inefficient and unaesthetic. The value should be computed only once, stored in a local object, and reused.

Guideline

Prefer precomputing values that won't change, instead of recreating objects unnecessarily.

Next, consider the way we increment `i` in the `for` loop:

```
for( /*...*/ ; i++ )
```

This temporary is more subtle, but it's easy to understand once you remember how preincrement and postincrement differ. Postincrement is usually less efficient than preincrement because it has to remember and return its original value. Postincrement for a class `T` should generally be implemented using the canonical form, as follows:

```
const T T::operator++(int)
{
  T old( *this ); // remember our original value
  ++*this;        // always implement postincrement
                  //   in terms of preincrement
  return old;     // return our original value
}
```

Now it's easy to see why postincrement is less efficient than preincrement. Postincrement has to do all the same work as preincrement, but in addition it also has to construct and return another object containing the original value.

Guideline

For consistency, always implement postincrement in terms of preincrement, otherwise your users will get surprising (and often unpleasant) results.

In the problem's code, the original value is never used, so there's no reason to use postincrement. Preincrement should be used instead. The accompanying box, "When Can Compilers Optimize Postincrement?" will tell you why compilers can't, in general, make the substitution for you automatically.

Guideline

Prefer preincrement. Only use postincrement if you're going to use the original value.

```
if( *i == name )
```

The `Employee` class isn't shown in the problem, but we can deduce a few things about it. For this code to work, `Employee` most likely has a conversion to `string` or a conversion constructor taking a `string`. Both cases create a temporary object, invoking either `operator==()` for `string`s or `operator==()` for `Employee`s (only if there does happen to be an `operator==()` that takes one of each, or `Employee` has a conversion to a reference—that is, `string&`—is a temporary not needed).

Guideline

Watch out for hidden temporaries created by implicit conversions. One good way to avoid this is to make constructors explicit when possible and avoid writing conversion operators.

When Can Compilers Optimize Postincrement?

Say you write a postincrement expression like "`i++`" but don't use the return value. Is the compiler allowed to notice this and simply rewrite the postincrement as preincrement as an optimization?

The answer is: No, not in general. The only time the compiler is allowed to optimize away unnecessary postincrement by rewriting it as preincrement is for builtin and standard types, such as `int` and `complex`, whose semantics the compiler is allowed to know because they're standard.

For class types, on the other hand, the compiler can't know the actual semantics of postincrement and preincrement—indeed, the two actually might not do the same thing. It would be a terrible thing indeed if the two functions didn't have the same semantics, and any programmer who wrote them with different semantics should be sacked on the spot. But, in general, that doesn't help the compiler, because it can't assume that the programmer is consistent.

There is a way you can deliberately let the compiler see the relationship between pre- and postincrement for a class type: Implement the canonical form of postincrement, which calls preincrement, and declare it `inline` so that the compiler can see across the function-call boundary (if it respects the `inline` directive) and detect the unused temporary object. I don't recommend this, because using `inline` is never a panacea, might be ignored by the compiler, and creates tighter coupling, among other issues. The much easier solution is simply to get in the habit of using preincrement if you're not going to use the original value, and then the above optimization will never be needed.

```
return i->addr;
return "";
```

This was one subtle red herring. It's true that both of these statements create temporary `string` objects, but those objects can't be avoided.

In the past, I've heard people argue that it's better to declare a local `string` object to hold the return value and have a single return statement that returns that `string` (`string ret; ... ret = i->addr; break; ... return ret;`). Although the single-entry/single-exit (SE/SE) discipline often makes for readable (and sometimes faster) code, whether it improves or degrades performance can depend greatly on your actual code and compiler.

In this case, the problem is that creating a single local `string` object and then assigning it would mean calling `string`'s default constructor and then possibly its assignment operator, instead of just a single constructor, as in our original code. "But," you ask, "how expensive could a plain old `string` default constructor be?" Well, here's how the "two-return" version performs on one popular compiler:

- With optimizations disabled: 5% faster than a return value `string` object
- With aggressive optimizations: 40% faster than a return value `string` object

```
string FindAddr( /*...*/ )
```

This was the second red herring. It may seem like you could avoid a temporary in all return cases simply by declaring the return type to be `string&` instead of `string`. Wrong! (In general; see the note below.) If you're lucky, your program will crash as soon as the calling code tries to use the reference, because the local object it refers to no longer exists. If you're unlucky, your code will appear to work and fail intermittently, causing you to spend long nights toiling away in the debugger.

> **Guideline**
>
> *Be aware of object lifetimes. Never, ever, ever return pointers or references to local automatic objects; they are completely unuseful because the calling code can't follow them, and (what's worse) the calling code might try.*

Although I won't pursue it further, I feel obliged to point out that there is a defensible option that allows returning a reference and thus avoiding a temporary. In brief:

```
const string&
FindAddr( /* pass emps and name by reference */ )
{
  for( /* ... */ )
  {
    if( i->name == name )
    {
      return i->addr;
    }
  }

  static const string empty;
  return empty;
}
```

Of course, the function's documentation must now define the valid lifetime of the reference. If the object is found, we are returning a reference to a `string` inside an `Employee` object inside the `list`, so the reference itself is only valid for the lifetime of the `Employee` object inside the list. Furthermore, the value of the string may change the next time the `Employee` object is changed.

I won't pursue this option further, because it often doesn't buy you much in practice, and because client programmers can be notoriously forgetful and careless about the lifetimes of the returned reference:

```
string& a = FindAddr( emps, "John Doe" );
emps.clear();
cout << a; // error
```

When the client programmer does something like this and uses a reference beyond its lifetime, the bug will typically be intermittent and very difficult to diagnose. Indeed, one of the most common mistakes programmers make with the standard library is to use iterators after they are no longer valid, which is pretty much the same thing as using a reference beyond its lifetime (see Item 1 for details about the accidental use of invalid iterators).

There are some other optimization opportunities. Ignoring these for now, here is a corrected version of `FindAddr` that fixes the unnecessary temporaries. Note that because the `list<Employee>` parameter is now `const`, the code has been changed to use `const_iterators`.

```
string FindAddr( const list<Employee>& emps,
                 const string&         name )
{
  list<Employee>::const_iterator end( emps.end() );
  for( list<Employee>::const_iterator i = emps.begin();
       i != end;
       ++i )
  {
    if( i->name == name )
    {
      return i->addr;
    }
  }
  return "";
}
```

Item 7: Using the Standard Library (or, Temporaries Revisited) Difficulty: 5

Effective reuse is an important part of good software engineering. To demonstrate how much better off you can be by using standard library algorithms instead of handcrafting your own, let's reconsider the previous Item to demonstrate how many of the problems could have been avoided by simply reusing what's already available in the standard library.

How many pitfalls in Item 6 could have been avoided if only the programmer had used a standard library algorithm instead of handcrafting the loop? Demonstrate. (As with Item 6, don't change the semantics of the function, even though they could be improved.)

To recap, here is the mostly-fixed function:

```
string FindAddr( const list<Employee>& emps,
                 const string&         name )
{
  list<Employee>::const_iterator end( emps.end() );
  for( list<Employee>::const_iterator i = emps.begin();
       i != end;
       ++i )
  {
    if( i->name == name )
    {
      return i->addr;
    }
  }
  return "";
}
```

Solution

With no other changes, simply using the standard `find()` algorithm could have avoided two temporaries, as well as the `emps.end()` recomputation inefficiency from the original code. For the best effect to reduce temporaries, provide an `operator==()` taking an `Employee&` and a name `string&`.

```
string FindAddr( list<Employee> emps, string name )
{
  list<Employee>::iterator i(
    find( emps.begin(), emps.end(), name )
    );
  if( i != emps.end() )
  {
    return i->addr;
  }
  return "";
}
```

Yes, you can get even fancier with functors and `find_if`, but see how much this simple reuse of `find` saves in programming effort and run-time efficiency.

Guideline

Reuse code—especially standard library code—instead of handcrafting your own. It's faster, easier, and safer.

Reusing existing code is usually preferable to handcrafting your own. The standard library is full of code that's intended to be used and reused, and to that end a lot of thought and care has gone into the design of the library, including its standard algorithms, such as `find()` and `sort()`. Implementers have spent hours sweating over efficiency details, usability details, all sorts of other considerations so that you don't have to. So reuse code, especially code in the standard library, and escape the trap of "I'll-write-my-own."

Combining this with the other fixes, we get a much improved function.

```
string FindAddr( const list<Employee>& emps,
                 const string&         name )
{
  list<Employee>::const_iterator i(
    find( emps.begin(), emps.end(), name )
    );
  if( i != emps.end() )
  {
    return i->addr;
  }
  return "";
}
```

Exception-Safety Issues and Techniques

First, a little of the history of this topic is in order. In 1994, Tom Cargill published the seminal article "Exception Handling: A False Sense of Security" (Cargill94).[1] It demonstrated conclusively that, at that time, the C++ community did not yet fully understand how to write exception-safe code. In fact, we didn't even know what all the important exception-safety issues were, or how to correctly reason about exception safety. Cargill challenged anyone to demonstrate a conclusive solution to this problem. Three years passed. A few people wrote partial responses to aspects of Cargill's example, but no one showed a comprehensive solution.

Then, in 1997, *Guru of the Week #8* appeared on the Internet newsgroup *comp.lang.c++.moderated*. Number 8 generated weeks of discussion and presented the first complete solution to Cargill's challenge. Later that year, a greatly expanded version that was updated to match the latest changes to draft standard C++ and demonstrating no fewer than three complete solutions, was published in the September and November/December issues of *C++ Report* under the title "Exception-Safe Generic Containers." (Copies of those original articles will also appear in the forthcoming book *C++ Gems II* [Martin00].)

In early 1999, on the *Effective C++ CD* (Meyers99), Scott Meyers included a recombined version of the articles, together with Cargill's original challenge, with the updated text of his classic books *Effective C++* and *More Effective C++*.

This miniseries has come a long way since its original publication as *Guru of the Week #8*. I hope you enjoy it and find it useful. Particular thanks go to fellow committee members Dave Abrahams and Greg Colvin for their insights into how to reason about exception-safety and their thoughtful critiques of several drafts of this material. Dave and Greg are, with Matt Austern, the authors of the two complete committee proposals for adding the current exception-safety guarantees into the standard library.

---

1. Available online at `http://www.gotw.ca/publications/xc++/sm_effective.htm`.

Item 8: Writing Exception-Safe Code—Part 1 Difficulty: 7

Exception handling and templates are two of C++'s most powerful features. Writing exception-safe code, however, can be difficult—especially in a template, when you may have no idea when (or what) a certain function might `throw` *your way.*

This miniseries tackles both major features, exception handling and templates, at once, by examining how to write exception-safe (works properly in the presence of exceptions) and exception-neutral (propagates all exceptions to the caller) generic containers. That's easy enough to say, but it's no mean feat.

So come on in, join the fun, and try your hand at implementing a simple container (a `Stack` that users can push and pop) and see the issues involved with making it exception-safe and exception-neutral.

We'll begin where Cargill left off—namely, by progressively creating a safe version of the `Stack` template he critiqued. Later on, we'll significantly improve the `Stack` container by reducing the requirements on `T`, the contained type, and show advanced techniques for managing resources exception-safely. Along the way, we'll find the answers to such questions as:

- What are the different "levels" of exception safety?
- Can or should generic containers be fully exception-neutral?
- Are the standard library containers exception-safe or exception-neutral?
- Does exception safety affect the design of your container's public interface?
- Should generic containers use exception specifications?

Here is the declaration of the `Stack` template, substantially the same as in Cargill's article. Your mission: Make `Stack` exception-safe and exception-neutral. That is, `Stack` objects should always be in a correct and consistent state, regardless of any exceptions that might be thrown in the course of executing `Stack`'s member functions. If any exceptions are thrown, they should be propagated seamlessly through to the caller, who can deal with them as he pleases, because he knows the context of `T` and we don't.

```
template <class T> class Stack
{
public:
  Stack();
  ~Stack();

  /*...*/

private:
  T*     v_;      // ptr to a memory area big
  size_t vsize_;  //  enough for 'vsize_' T's
  size_t vused_;  // # of T's actually in use
};
```

Write the `Stack` default constructor and destructor in a way that is demonstrably exception-safe (works properly in the presence of exceptions) and exception-neutral (propagates all exceptions to the caller, without causing integrity problems in a `Stack` object).

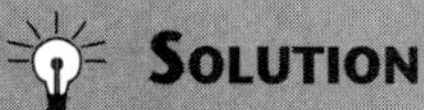

SOLUTION

Right away, we can see that `Stack` is going to have to manage dynamic memory resources. Clearly, one key is going to be avoiding leaks, even in the presence of exceptions thrown by `T` operations and standard memory allocations. For now, we'll manage these memory resources within each `Stack` member function. Later on in this miniseries, we'll improve on this by using a private base class to encapsulate resource ownership.

Default Construction

First, consider one possible default constructor:

```
// Is this safe?

template<class T>
Stack<T>::Stack()
  : v_(0),
    vsize_(10),
    vused_(0)          // nothing used yet
{
  v_ = new T[vsize_]; // initial allocation
}
```

Is this constructor exception-safe and exception-neutral? To find out, consider what might throw. In short, the answer is: any function. So the first step is to analyze this code and determine which functions will actually be called, including both free functions and constructors, destructors, operators, and other member functions.

This `Stack` constructor first sets `vsize_` to 10, then attempts to allocate some initial memory using `new T[vsize_]`. The latter first tries to call `operator new[]()` (either the default `operator new[]()` or one provided by `T`) to allocate the memory, then tries to call `T::T` a total of `vsize_` times. There are two operations that might fail. First, the memory allocation itself, in which case `operator new[]()` will throw a `bad_alloc` exception. Second, `T`'s default constructor, which might throw anything at all, in which case any objects that were constructed are destroyed and the allocated memory is automatically guaranteed to be deallocated via `operator delete[]()`.

Hence the above function is fully exception-safe and exception-neutral, and we can move on to the next...what? Why is the function fully robust, you ask? All right, let's examine it in a little more detail.

1. *We're exception-neutral.* We don't catch anything, so if the `new` throws, then the exception is correctly propagated up to our caller as required.

> **Guideline**
>
> *If a function isn't going to handle (or translate or deliberately absorb) an exception, it should allow the exception to propagate up to a caller who can handle it.*

2. *We don't leak.* If the `operator new[]()` allocation call exited by throwing a `bad_alloc` exception, then no memory was allocated to begin with, so there can't be a leak. If one of the `T` constructors threw, then any `T` objects that were fully constructed were properly destroyed and, finally, `operator delete[]()` was automatically called to release the memory. That makes us leakproof, as advertised.

I'm ignoring for now the possibility that one of the `T` destructor calls might throw during the cleanup, which would call `terminate()` and simply kill the program altogether and leave events well out of your control anyway. See the point in Item 16 in which we cover information on "destructors that throw and why they're evil."

3. *We're in a consistent state whether or not any part of the `new` throws.* Now one might think that if the `new` throws, then `vsize_` has already been set to 10 when, in fact, nothing was successfully allocated. Isn't that inconsistent? Not really, because it's irrelevant. Remember, if the `new` throws, we propagate the exception out of our own constructor, right? And, by definition, "exiting a constructor by means of an exception" means our `Stack` proto-object never actually got to become a completely constructed object at all. Its lifetime never started, so its state is meaningless because the object never existed. It doesn't matter what the memory that briefly held `vsize_` was set to, any more than it matters what the memory was set to after we leave an object's destructor. All that's left is raw memory, smoke, and ashes.

> **Guideline**
>
> *Always structure your code so that resources are correctly freed and data is in a consistent state even in the presence of exceptions.*

All right, I'll admit it: I put the `new` in the constructor body purely to open the door for that third discussion. What I'd actually prefer to write is:

```
template<class T>
Stack<T>::Stack()
  : v_(new T[10]),  // default allocation
    vsize_(10),
    vused_(0)       // nothing used yet
{
}
```

Both versions are practically equivalent. I prefer the latter because it follows the usual good practice of initializing members in initializer lists whenever possible.

Destruction

The destructor looks a lot easier, once we make a (greatly) simplifying assumption.

```
template<class T>
Stack<T>::~Stack()
{
  delete[] v_;        // this can't throw
}
```

Why can't the `delete[]` call throw? Recall that this invokes `T::~T` for each object in the array, then calls `operator delete[]()` to deallocate the memory. We know that the deallocation by `operator delete[]()` may never throw, because the standard requires that its signature is always one of the following:[2]

```
void operator delete[]( void* ) throw();
void operator delete[]( void*, size_t ) throw();
```

Hence, the only thing that could possibly throw is one of the `T::~T` calls, and we're arbitrarily going to have `Stack` require that `T::~T` may not throw. Why? To make a long story short, we just can't implement the `Stack` destructor with complete exception safety if `T::~T` can throw, that's why. However, requiring that `T::~T` may not throw isn't particularly onerous, because there are plenty of other reasons why destructors should never be allowed to throw at all.[3] Any class whose destructor can throw is likely to cause you all sorts of other problems sooner or later, and you can't even reliably `new[]` or `delete[]` an array of them. More on that as we continue in this miniseries.

Guideline

Observe the canonical exception safety rules: Never allow an exception to escape from a destructor or from an `overloaded operator delete()` or `operator delete[]()`; write every destructor and deallocation function as though it had an exception specification of "`throw()`". More on this as we go on; this is an important theme.

2. As Scott Meyers pointed out in private communication, strictly speaking this doesn't prevent someone from providing an overloaded `operator delete[]` that does throw, but any such overload would violate this clear intent and should be considered defective.
3. Frankly, you won't go far wrong if you habitually write `throw()` after the declaration of every destructor you ever write. Even if exception specifications cause expensive checks under your current compiler, at least write all your destructors as though they were specified as `throw()`—that is, never allow exceptions to leave destructors.

Item 9: Writing Exception-Safe Code—Part 2 Difficulty: 8

Now that we have the default constructor and the destructor under our belts, we might be tempted to think that all the other functions will be about the same. Well, writing exception-safe and exception-neutral copy and assignment code presents its own challenges, as we shall now see.

Consider again Cargill's `Stack` template:

```
template <class T> class Stack
{
public:
  Stack();
  ~Stack();
  Stack(const Stack&);
  Stack& operator=(const Stack&);
  /*...*/
private:
  T*     v_;      // ptr to a memory area big
  size_t vsize_;  //  enough for 'vsize_' T's
  size_t vused_;  // # of T's actually in use
};
```

Now write the `Stack` copy constructor and copy assignment operator so that both are demonstrably exception-safe (work properly in the presence of exceptions) and exception-neutral (propagate all exceptions to the caller, without causing integrity problems in a `Stack` object).

Solution

To implement the copy constructor and the copy assignment operator, let's use a common helper function, `NewCopy`, to manage allocating and growing memory. `NewCopy` takes a pointer to (`src`) and size of (`srcsize`) an existing `T` buffer, and returns a pointer to a new and possibly larger copy of the buffer, passing ownership of the new buffer to the caller. If exceptions are encountered, `NewCopy` correctly releases all temporary resources and propagates the exception in such a way that nothing is leaked.

```
template<class T>
T* NewCopy( const T* src,
            size_t   srcsize,
            size_t   destsize )
{
  assert( destsize >= srcsize );
  T* dest = new T[destsize];
  try
  {
    copy( src, src+srcsize, dest );
  }
```

```
  catch(...)
  {
    delete[] dest; // this can't throw
    throw;         // rethrow original exception
  }
  return dest;
}
```

Let's analyze this one step at a time.

1. In the `new` statement, the allocation might throw `bad_alloc` or the `T::T`'s may throw anything. In either case, nothing is allocated and we simply allow the exception to propagate. This is both leak-free and exception-neutral.

2. Next, we assign all the existing values using `T::operator=()`. If any of the assignments fail, we catch the exception, free the allocated memory, and rethrow the original exception. This is again both leak-free and exception-neutral. However, there's an important subtlety here: `T::operator=()` must guarantee that if it does throw, then the assigned-to `T` object must be destructible.[4]

3. If the allocation and copy both succeed, then we return the pointer to the new buffer and relinquish ownership (that is, the caller is responsible for the buffer from here on out). The return simply copies the pointer value, which cannot throw.

Copy Construction

With `NewCopy` in hand, the `Stack` copy constructor is easy to write.

```
template<class T>
Stack<T>::Stack( const Stack<T>& other )
  : v_(NewCopy( other.v_,
                other.vsize_,
                other.vsize_ )),
    vsize_(other.vsize_),
    vused_(other.vused_)
{
}
```

The only possible exception is from `NewCopy`, which manages its own resources.

Copy Assignment

Next, we tackle copy assignment.

```
template<class T>
Stack<T>&
Stack<T>::operator=( const Stack<T>& other )
```

4. As we progress, we'll arrive at an improved version of `Stack` that does not rely on `T::operator=`.

```
{
  if( this != &other )
  {
    T* v_new = NewCopy( other.v_,
                        other.vsize_,
                        other.vsize_ );
    delete[] v_;  // this can't throw
    v_ = v_new;   // take ownership
    vsize_ = other.vsize_;
    vused_ = other.vused_;
  }
  return *this;   // safe, no copy involved
}
```

Again, after the routine weak guard against self-assignment, only the `NewCopy` call might throw. If it does, we correctly propagate that exception, without affecting the `Stack` object's state. To the caller, if the assignment throws then the state is unchanged, and if the assignment doesn't throw, then the assignment and all its side effects are successful and complete.

What we see here is the following very important exception-safety idiom.

> **Guideline**
>
> *Observe the canonical exception-safety rules: In each function, take all the code that might emit an exception and do all that work safely off to the side. Only then, when you know that the real work has succeeded, should you modify the program state (and clean up) using only non-throwing operations.*

Item 10: Writing Exception-Safe Code—Part 3 Difficulty: $9\frac{1}{2}$

Are you getting the hang of exception safety? Well, then, it must be time to throw you a curve ball. So get ready, and don't swing too soon.

Now for the final piece of Cargill's original `Stack` template.

```
template <class T> class Stack
{
public:
  Stack();
  ~Stack();
  Stack(const Stack&);
  Stack& operator=(const Stack&);
  size_t Count() const;
  void   Push(const T&);
  T      Pop();   // if empty, throws exception
```

```
private:
  T*     v_;      // ptr to a memory area big
  size_t vsize_;  //  enough for 'vsize_' T's
  size_t vused_;  // # of T's actually in use
};
```

Write the final three Stack functions: Count(), Push(), and Pop(). Remember, be exception-safe and exception-neutral!

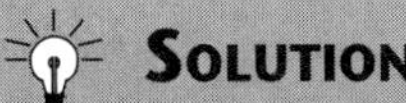

Count()

The easiest of all Stack's members to implement safely is Count, because all it does is copy a builtin that can never throw.

```
template<class T>
size_t Stack<T>::Count() const
{
  return vused_;  // safe, builtins don't throw
}
```

No problem.

Push()

On the other hand, with Push, we need to apply our now-usual duty of care.

```
template<class T>
void Stack<T>::Push( const T& t )
{
  if( vused_ == vsize_ )  // grow if necessary
  {                       // by some grow factor
    size_t vsize_new = vsize_*2+1;
    T* v_new = NewCopy( v_, vsize_, vsize_new );
    delete[] v_;  // this can't throw
    v_ = v_new;   // take ownership
    vsize_ = vsize_new;
  }
  v_[vused_] = t;
  ++vused_;
}
```

If we have no more space, we first pick a new size for the buffer and make a larger copy using NewCopy. Again, if NewCopy throws, then our own Stack's state is unchanged and the exception propagates through cleanly. Deleting the original buffer and taking ownership of the new one involves only operations that are known not to throw, so the entire `if` block is exception-safe.

After any required grow operation, we attempt to copy the new value before incrementing our `vused_` count. This way, if the assignment throws, the increment is not performed and our `Stack`'s state is unchanged. If the assignment succeeds, the `Stack`'s state is changed to recognize the presence of the new value, and all is well.

> **Guideline**
>
> *Observe the canonical exception-safety rules: In each function, take all the code that might emit an exception and do all that work safely off to the side; only then, when you know that the real work has succeeded, should you modify the program state (and clean up) using only non-throwing operations.*

Pop() Goes the Weasel

Only one function left. That wasn't so hard, was it? Well, don't get too happy yet, because it turns out that `Pop` is the most problematic of these functions to write with complete exception safety. Our initial attempt might look something like this:

```
// Hmmm... how safe is it really?

template<class T>
T Stack<T>::Pop()
{
  if( vused_ == 0)
  {
    throw "pop from empty stack";
  }
  else
  {
    T result = v_[vused_-1];
    --vused_;
    return result;
  }
}
```

If the stack is empty, we throw an appropriate exception. Otherwise, we create a copy of the `T` object to be returned, update our state, and return the `T` object. If the initial copy from `v_[vused_-1]` fails, the exception is propagated and the state of the `Stack` is unchanged, which is what we want. If the initial copy succeeds, our state is updated and the `Stack` is in its new consistent state, which is also what we want.

So this works, right? Well, kind of. There is a subtle flaw here that's completely outside the purview of `Stack::Pop()`. Consider the following client code:

```
string s1(s.Pop());
string s2;
s2 = s.Pop();
```

Note that above we talked about "the initial copy" (from v_[vused_-1]). That's because there is another copy[5] to worry about in either of the above cases—namely, the copy of the returned temporary into the destination. If that copy construction or copy assignment fails, then the Stack has completed its side effect (the top element has been popped off), but the popped value is now lost forever, because it never reached its destination (oops). This is bad news. In effect, it means that any version of Pop() that is written to return a temporary like this—and that therefore is responsible for two side effects—cannot be made completely exception-safe, because even though the function's implementation itself may look technically exception-safe, it forces clients of Stack to write exception-unsafe code. More generally, mutator functions should not return T objects by value. (See Item 19 for more about exception-safety issues for functions with multiple side effects.)

The bottom line—and it's significant—is this: *Exception safety affects your class's design.* In other words, you must design for exception safety from the outset, and exception safety is never "just an implementation detail."

> **Common Mistake**
>
> *Never make exception safety an afterthought. Exception safety affects a class's design. It is never "just an implementation detail."*

The Real Problem

One alternative—in fact, the minimum possible change[6]—is to respecify Pop as follows:

```
template<class T>
void Stack<T>::Pop( T& result )
{
  if( vused_ == 0)
  {
    throw "pop from empty stack";
  }
  else
  {
    result = v_[vused_-1];
    --vused_;
  }
}
```

5. For you experienced readers, yes, it's actually "zero or one copies," because the compiler is free to optimize away the second copy if the return value optimization applies. The point is that there can be a copy, so you have to be ready for it.
6. The minimum possible *acceptable* change, that is. You could always simply change the original version to return T& instead of T (this would be a reference to the popped T object, because for the time being the popped object happens to still physically exist in your internal representation), and then the caller could still write exception-safe code. But this business of returning references to "I no longer consider it there" resources is purely evil. If you change your implementation in the future, this may no longer be possible! Don't go there.

This ensures that the Stack's state is not changed unless the copy safely arrives in the caller's hands.

But the real problem is that, as specified, Pop() has *two* responsibilities—namely, to pop the top-most element and to return the just-popped value.

> **Guideline**
>
> *Prefer cohesion. Always endeavor to give each piece of code—each module, each class, each function—a single, well-defined responsibility.*

So another option (and preferable, in my opinion) is to separate the functions of "querying the top-most value" and "popping the top-most value off the stack." We do this by having one function for each.

```
template<class T>
T& Stack<T>::Top()
{
  if( vused_ == 0)
  {
    throw "empty stack";
  }
  return v_[vused_-1];
}

template<class T>
void Stack<T>::Pop()
{
  if( vused_ == 0)
  {
    throw "pop from empty stack";
  }
  else
  {
    --vused_;
  }
}
```

Incidentally, have you ever grumbled at the way the standard library containers' pop functions (for example, list::pop_back, stack::pop, etc.) don't return the popped value? Well, here's one reason to do this: It avoids weakening exception safety.

In fact, you've probably noticed that the above separated Top and Pop now match the signatures of the top and pop members of the standard library's stack<> adapter. That's no coincidence. We're actually only two public member functions away from the stack<> adapter's full public interface—namely:

```
template<class T>
const T& Stack<T>::Top() const
{
  if( vused_ == 0)
  {
    throw "empty stack";
```

```
    }
    else
    {
      return v_[vused_-1];
    }
  }
```

to provide Top for const Stack objects, and:

```
template<class T>
bool Stack<T>::Empty() const
{
  return( vused_ == 0 );
}
```

Of course, the standard stack<> is actually a container adapter that's implemented in terms of another container, but the public interface is the same and the rest is just an implementation detail.

There's just one more fundamental point I want to drive home. I'll leave the following with you to ponder.

> **Common Mistake**
>
> *"Exception-unsafe" and "poor design" go hand in hand. If a piece of code isn't exception-safe, that's generally okay and can simply be fixed. But if a piece of code cannot be made exception-safe because of its underlying design, that almost always is a signal of its poor design. Example 1: A function with two different responsibilities is difficult to make exception-safe. Example 2: A copy assignment operator that is written in such a way that it must check for self-assignment is probably not strongly exception-safe either*

You will see Example 2 demonstrated very soon in this miniseries. Note that copy assignment operators may well elect to check for self-assignment even if they don't have to—for example, they might do so for efficiency. But a copy assignment operator that *has* to check for self-assignment (and else would not work correctly for self-assignment) is probably not strongly exception-safe.

Item 11: Writing Exception-Safe Code—Part 4 Difficulty: 8

Mid-series interlude: What have we accomplished so far?

Now that we have implemented an exception-safe and exception-neutral Stack<T>, answer these questions as precisely as possible:

1. What are the important exception-safety guarantees?
2. For the Stack<T> that was just implemented, what are the requirements on T, the contained type?

SOLUTION

Just as there's more than one way to skin a cat (I have a feeling I'm going to get enraged e-mail from animal lovers), there's more than one way to write exception-safe code. In fact, there are two main alternatives we can choose from when it comes to guaranteeing exception safety. These guarantees were first set out in this form by Dave Abrahams.

1. *Basic guarantee: Even in the presence of exceptions thrown by `T` or other exceptions, `Stack` objects don't leak resources.* Note that this also implies that the container will be destructible and usable even if an exception is thrown while performing some container operation. However, if an exception is thrown, the container will be in a consistent, but not necessarily predictable, state. Containers that support the basic guarantee can work safely in some settings.

2. *Strong guarantee: If an operation terminates because of an exception, program state will remain unchanged.* This always implies commit-or-rollback semantics, including that no references or iterators into the container be invalidated if an operation fails. For example, if a `Stack` client calls `Top` and then attempts a `Push` that fails because of an exception, then the state of the `Stack` object must be unchanged and the reference returned from the prior call to `Top` must still be valid. For more information on these guarantees, see Dave Abrahams's documentation of the SGI exception-safe standard library adaptation at: `http://www.gotw.ca/publications/xc++/da_stlsafety.htm`.

Probably the most interesting point here is that when you implement the basic guarantee, the strong guarantee often comes along for free.[7] For example, in our `Stack` implementation, almost everything we did was needed to satisfy just the basic guarantee—and what's presented above very nearly satisfies the strong guarantee, with little or no extra work.[8] Not half bad, considering all the trouble we went to.

In addition to these two guarantees, there is one more guarantee that certain functions must provide in order to make overall exception safety possible:

3. *Nothrow guarantee: The function will not emit an exception under any circumstances.* Overall exception safety isn't possible unless certain functions are guaranteed not to

7. Note that I said "often," not "always." In the standard library, for example, `vector` is a well-known counter-example in which satisfying the basic guarantee does not cause the strong guarantee to come along for free.

8. There is one subtle way in which this version of `Stack` still falls short of the strong guarantee. If `Push()` is called and has to grow its internal buffer, but then its final `v_[vused_] = t;` assignment throws, the `Stack` is still in a consistent state, but its internal memory buffer has moved—which invalidates any previously valid references returned from `Top()`. This last flaw in `Stack::Push()` can be fixed fairly easily by moving some code and adding a `try` block. For a better solution, however, see the `Stack` presented in the second half of this miniseries. That `Stack` does not have the problem, and it does satisfy the strong commit-or-rollback guarantee.

throw. In particular, we've seen that this is true for destructors; later in this miniseries, we'll see that it's also needed in certain helper functions, such as `Swap()`.

Guideline

Understand the basic, strong, and nothrow exception-safety guarantees.

Now we have some points to ponder. Note that we've been able to implement `Stack` to be not only exception-safe but fully exception-neutral, yet we've used only a single `try/catch`. As we'll see next time, using better encapsulation techniques can get rid of even this `try` block. That means we can write a strongly exception-safe and exception-neutral generic container, without using `try` or `catch`—very natty, very elegant.

For the template as we've seen it so far, `Stack` requires its instantiation type to have all of the following:

- Default constructor (to construct the `v_` buffers)
- Copy constructor (if `Pop` returns by value)
- Nonthrowing destructor (to be able to guarantee exception-safety)
- *Exception-safe* copy assignment (To set the values in `v_`, and if the copy assignment throws, then it must guarantee that the target object is still a valid `T`. Note that this is the only `T` member function that must be exception-safe in order for our `Stack` to be exception-safe.)

In the second half of this miniseries, we'll also see how to reduce even these requirements, without compromising exception safety. Along the way, we'll get an even more-detailed look at the standard operation of the statement `delete[] x;`.

Item 12: Writing Exception-Safe Code—Part 5 Difficulty: 7

All right, you've had enough rest—roll up your sleeves, and get ready for a wild ride.

Now we're ready to delve a little deeper into the same example, and write not just one but two new-and-improved versions of `Stack`. Not only is it, indeed, possible to write exception-safe generic containers, but by the time this miniseries is over, we'll have created no fewer than three complete solutions to the exception-safe `Stack` problem.

Along the way, we'll also discover the answers to several more interesting questions:

- How can we use more-advanced techniques to simplify the way we manage resources and get rid of the last `try/catch` into the bargain?
- How can we improve `Stack` by reducing the requirements on `T`, the contained type?
- Should generic containers use exception specifications?
- What do `new[]` and `delete[]` really do?

The answer to the last question may be quite different from what one might expect. Writing exception-safe containers in C++ isn't rocket science; it just requires significant care and a good understanding of how the language works. In particular, it helps to develop a habit of eyeing with mild suspicion anything that might turn out to be a function call—including user-defined operators, user-defined conversions, and silent temporary objects among the more subtle culprits—because any function call might throw.[9]

One way to greatly simplify an exception-safe container like `Stack` is to use better encapsulation. Specifically, we'd like to encapsulate the basic memory management work. Most of the care we had to take while writing our original exception-safe `Stack` was needed just to get the basic memory allocation right, so let's introduce a simple helper class to put all that work in one place.

```
template <class T> class StackImpl
{
/*????*/:
  StackImpl(size_t size=0);
  ~StackImpl();
  void Swap(StackImpl& other) throw();

  T*     v_;       // ptr to a memory area big
  size_t vsize_;   //  enough for 'vsize_' T's
  size_t vused_;   // # of T's actually in use

private:
  // private and undefined: no copying allowed
  StackImpl( const StackImpl& );
  StackImpl& operator=( const StackImpl& );
};
```

Note that `StackImpl` has all the original `Stack`'s data members so that we've essentially moved the original `Stack`'s representation entirely into `StackImpl`. `StackImpl` also has a helper function named `Swap`, which exchanges the guts of our `StackImpl` object with those of another `StackImpl`.

Your tasks:

1. Implement all three member functions of `StackImpl`, but not just any old way. Assume that at any time, the `v_` buffer must contain exactly as many constructed `T` objects as there are `T` objects in the container, no more, no less. In particular, unused space in the `v_` buffer should not contain constructed `T` objects.
2. Describe `StackImpl`'s responsibilities. Why does it exist?
3. What should `/*????*/` be? How does the choice affect how `StackImpl` will be used? Be as specific as possible.

---

9. Except for functions declared with an exception specification of `throw()` or certain functions in the standard library that are documented to never throw.

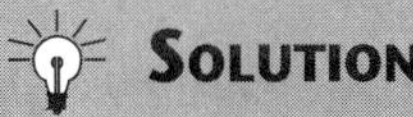

Solution

We won't spend much time analyzing why the following functions are fully exception-safe (work properly in the presence of exceptions) and exception-neutral (propagate all exceptions to the caller), because the reasons are pretty much the same as those we discussed in detail in the first half of this miniseries. But do take a few minutes now to analyze these solutions, and note the commentary.

Constructor

The constructor is fairly straightforward. We'll use `operator new()` to allocate the buffer as raw memory. (Note that if we used a new-expression like `new T[size]`, then the buffer would be initialized to default-constructed `T` objects, which was explicitly disallowed in the problem statement.)

```
template <class T>
StackImpl<T>::StackImpl( size_t size )
  : v_( static_cast<T*>
          ( size == 0
            ? 0
            : operator new(sizeof(T)*size) ) ),
    vsize_(size),
    vused_(0)
{
}
```

Destructor

The destructor is the easiest of the three functions to implement. Again, remember what we learned about `operator delete()` earlier in this miniseries. (See "Some Standard Helper Functions" for full details about functions such as `destroy()` and `swap()` that appear in the next few pieces of code.)

```
template <class T>
StackImpl<T>::~StackImpl()
{
    destroy( v_, v_+vused_ ); // this can't throw
    operator delete( v_ );
}
```

We'll see what `destroy()` is in a moment.

Some Standard Helper Functions

The Stack and StackImpl presented in this solution use three helper functions, one of which (swap()) also appears in the standard library: construct(), destroy(), and swap(). In simplified form, here's what these functions look like:

```
// construct() constructs a new object in
// a given location using an initial value
//
template <class T1, class T2>
void construct( T1* p, const T2& value )
{
  new (p) T1(value);
}
```

The above form of new is called "placement new," and instead of allocating memory for the new object, it just puts it into the memory pointed at by p. Any object new'd in this way should generally be destroyed by calling its destructor explicitly (as in the following two functions), rather than by using delete.

```
// destroy() destroys an object or a range
// of objects
//
template <class T>
void destroy( T* p )
{
  p->~T();
}
template <class FwdIter>
void destroy( FwdIter first, FwdIter last )
{
  while( first != last )
  {
    destroy( &*first );
    ++first;
  }
}
// swap() just exchanges two values
//
template <class T>
void swap( T& a, T& b )
{
  T temp(a); a = b; b = temp;
}
```

Of these, destroy(first,last) is the most interesting. We'll return to it a little later in the main miniseries; it illustrates more than one might think!

Swap

Finally, a simple but very important function. Believe it or not, this is the function that is instrumental in making the complete `Stack` class so elegant, especially its `operator=()`, as we'll see soon.

```
template <class T>
void StackImpl<T>::Swap(StackImpl& other) throw()
{
    swap( v_,     other.v_ );
    swap( vsize_, other.vsize_ );
    swap( vused_, other.vused_ );
}
```

To picture how `Swap()` works, say that you have two `StackImpl<T>` objects `a` and `b`, as shown in Figure 1.

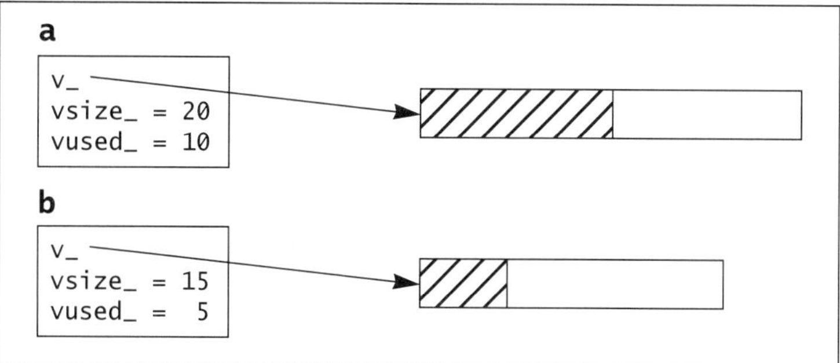

Figure 1: Two `StackImpl<T>` objects `a` and `b`

Then executing `a.Swap(b)` changes the state to that shown in Figure 2.

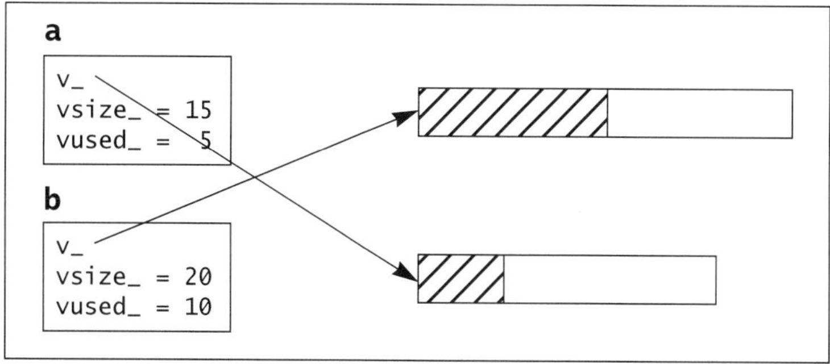

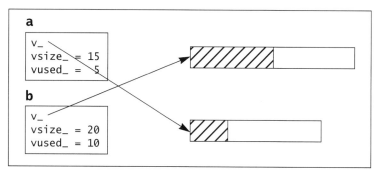

Figure 2: The same two `StackImpl<T>` objects, after `a.Swap(b)`

Note that Swap() supports the strongest exception guarantee of all—namely, the nothrow guarantee; Swap() is guaranteed not to throw an exception under any circumstances. It turns out that this feature of Swap() is essential, a linchpin in the chain of reasoning about Stack's own exception safety.

Why does StackImpl exist? Well, there's nothing magical going on here: StackImpl is responsible for simple raw memory management and final cleanup, so any class that uses it won't have to worry about those details.

> **Guideline**
>
> *Prefer cohesion. Always endeavor to give each piece of code—each module, each class, each function—a single, well-defined responsibility.*

So what access specifier would you write in place of the comment "/*????*/"? Hint: The name StackImpl itself hints at some kind of "implemented-in-terms-of" relationship, and there are two main ways to write that kind of relationship in C++.

*Technique 1: Private Base Class.*The missing /*????*/ access specifier must be either protected or public. (If it were private, no one could use the class.) First, consider what happens if we make it protected.

Using protected means that StackImpl is intended to be used as a private base class. So Stack will be "implemented in terms of" StackImpl, which is what private inheritance means, and we have a clear division of responsibilities. The StackImpl base class will take care of managing the memory buffer and destroying all remaining T objects during Stack destruction, while the Stack derived class will take care of constructing all T objects within the raw memory. The raw memory management takes place pretty much entirely outside Stack itself, because, for example, the initial allocation must fully succeed before any Stack constructor body can be entered. Item 13 begins the final phase of this miniseries, in which we'll concentrate on implementing this version.

Technique 2: Private Member. Next, consider what happens if StackImpl's missing /*????*/ access specifier is public.

Using public hints that StackImpl is intended to be used as a struct by some external client, because its data members are public. So again, Stack will be "implemented in terms of" StackImpl, only this time using a HAS-A containment relationship instead of private inheritance. We still have the same clear division of responsibilities. The StackImpl object will take care of managing the memory buffer and destroying all T objects remaining during Stack destruction, and the containing Stack will take care of constructing T objects within the raw memory. Because data members are initialized before a class's constructor body is entered, the raw memory management still takes place pretty much entirely outside Stack, because, for example, the initial allocation must fully succeed before any Stack constructor body can be entered.

As we'll see when we look at the code, this second technique is only slightly different from the first.

Item 13: Writing Exception-Safe Code—Part 6 Difficulty: 9

And now for an even better `Stack`*, with fewer requirements on* `T`*—not to mention a very elegant* `operator=()`.

Imagine that the `/*????*/` comment in `StackImpl` stood for `protected`. Implement all the member functions of the following version of `Stack`, which is to be implemented in terms of `StackImpl` by using `StackImpl` as a private base class.

```
template <class T>
class Stack : private StackImpl<T>
{
public:
  Stack(size_t size=0);
  ~Stack();
  Stack(const Stack&);
  Stack& operator=(const Stack&);
  size_t Count() const;
  void   Push(const T&);
  T&     Top();    // if empty, throws exception
  void   Pop();    // if empty, throws exception
};
```

As always, remember to make all the functions exception-safe and exception-neutral.

(Hint: There's a very elegant way to implement a fully safe `operator=()`. Can you spot it?)

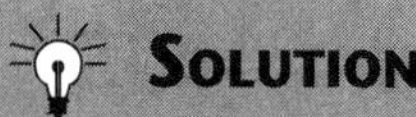

Solution

The Default Constructor

Using the private base class method, our `Stack` class will look something like this (the code is shown inlined for brevity):

```
template <class T>
class Stack : private StackImpl<T>
{
public:
  Stack(size_t size=0)
    : StackImpl<T>(size)
  {
  }
```

Stack's default constructor simply calls the default constructor of StackImpl, that just sets the stack's state to empty and optionally performs an initial allocation. The only operation here that might throw is the new done in StackImpl's constructor, and that's unimportant when considering Stack's own exception safety. If it does happen, we won't enter the Stack constructor body and there will never have been a Stack object at all, so any initial allocation failures in the base class don't affect Stack. (See Item 8, and *More Exceptional C++* Items 17 and 18, for additional comments about exiting constructors via an exception.)

Note that we slightly changed Stack's original constructor interface to allow a starting "hint" at the amount of memory to allocate. We'll make use of this in a minute when we write the Push function.

> **Guideline**
>
> *Observe the canonical exception-safety rules: Always use the "resource acquisition is initialization" idiom to isolate resource ownership and management.*

The Destructor

Here's the first elegance: We don't need to provide a Stack destructor. The default compiler-generated Stack destructor is fine, because it just calls the StackImpl destructor to destroy any objects that were constructed and actually free the memory. Elegant.

The Copy Constructor

Note that the Stack copy constructor does not call the StackImpl copy constructor. (See the previous solution for a discussion of what construct() does.)

```
Stack(const Stack& other)
  : StackImpl<T>(other.vused_)
{
  while( vused_ < other.vused_ )
  {
    construct( v_+vused_, other.v_[vused_] );
    ++vused_;
  }
}
```

Copy construction is now efficient and clean. The worst that can happen here is that a T constructor could fail, in which case the StackImpl destructor will correctly destroy exactly as many objects as were successfully created and then deallocate the raw memory. One big benefit derived from StackImpl is that we could add as many more constructors as we want without putting clean-up code inside each one.

Elegant Copy Assignment

The following is an incredibly elegant and nifty way to write a completely safe copy assignment operator. It's even cooler if you've never seen the technique before.

```
Stack& operator=(const Stack& other)
{
  Stack temp(other); // does all the work
  Swap( temp );      // this can't throw
  return *this;
}
```

Do you get it? Take a minute to think about it before reading on.

This function is the epitome of a very important guideline that we've seen already.

> **Guideline**
>
> *Observe the canonical exception-safety rules: In each function, take all the code that might emit an exception and do all that work safely off to the side. Only then, when you know that the real work has succeeded, should you modify the program state (and clean up) using only non-throwing operations.*

It's beautifully elegant, if a little subtle. We just construct a temporary object from `other`, then call `Swap` to swap our own guts with `temp`'s, and, finally, when `temp` goes out of scope and destroys itself, it automatically cleans up our old guts in the process, leaving us with the new state.

Note that when `operator=()` is made exception-safe like this, a side effect is that it also automatically handles self-assignment (for example, `Stack s; s = s;`) correctly without further work. (Because self-assignment is exceedingly rare, I omitted the traditional `if( this != &other )` test, which has its own subtleties. See Item 38 for all the gory details.)

Note that because all the real work is done while constructing `temp`, any exceptions that might be thrown (either by memory allocation or `T` copy construction) can't affect the state of our object. Also, there won't be any memory leaks or other problems from the `temp` object, because the `Stack` copy constructor is already strongly exception-safe. Once all the work is done, we simply swap our object's internal representation with `temp`'s, which cannot throw (because `Swap` has a `throw()` exception specification, and because it does nothing but copy builtins), and we're done.

Note especially how much more elegant this is than the exception-safe copy assignment we implemented in Item 9. This version also requires much less care to ensure that it's been made properly exception-safe.

If you're one of those folks who like terse code, you can write the operator=() canonical form more compactly by using pass-by-value to create the temporary:

```
Stack& operator=(Stack temp)
{
  Swap( temp );
  return *this;
}
```

Stack<T>::Count()

Yes, Count() is still the easiest member function to write.

```
size_t Count() const
{
  return vused_;
}
```

Stack<T>::Push()

Push() needs a little more attention. Study it for a moment before reading on.

```
void Push( const T& t )
{
  if( vused_ == vsize_ )  // grow if necessary
  {
    Stack temp( vsize_*2+1 );
    while( temp.Count() < vused_ )
    {
      temp.Push( v_[temp.Count()] );
    }
    temp.Push( t );
    Swap( temp );
  }
  else
  {
    construct( v_+vused_, t );
    ++vused_;
  }
}
```

First, consider the simple else case: If we already have room for the new object, we attempt to construct it. If the construction succeeds, we update our vused_ count. This is safe and straightforward.

Otherwise, like last time, if we don't have enough room for the new element, we trigger a reallocation. In this case, we simply construct a temporary Stack object, push the new element onto that, and finally swap out our original guts to it to ensure they're disposed of in a tidy fashion.

But is this exception-safe? Yes. Consider:

- If the construction of temp fails, our state is unchanged and no resources have been leaked, so that's fine.
- If any part of the loading of `temp`'s contents (including the new object's copy construction) fails by throwing an exception, `temp` is properly cleaned up when its destructor is called as `temp` goes out of scope.
- In no case do we alter our state until all the work has already been completed successfully.

Note that this provides the strong commit-or-rollback guarantee, because the `Swap()` is performed only if the entire reallocate-and-push operation succeeds. Any references returned from `Top()`, or iterators if we later chose to provide them, would never be invalidated (by a possible internal grow operation) if the insertion is not completely successful.

`Stack<T>::Top()`

`Top()` hasn't changed at all.

```
    T& Top()
    {
      if( vused_ == 0 )
      {
        throw "empty stack";
      }
      return v_[vused_-1];
    }
```

`Stack<T>::Pop()`

Neither has `Pop()`, save the new call to `destroy()`.

```
    void Pop()
    {
      if( vused_ == 0 )
      {
        throw "pop from empty stack";
      }
      else
      {
        --vused_;
        destroy( v_+vused_ );
      }
    }
  };
```

In summary, `Push()` has been simplified, but the biggest benefit of encapsulating the resource ownership in a separate class was seen in `Stack`'s constructor and destructor.

Thanks to `StackImpl`, we can go on to write as many more constructors as we like, without having to worry about clean-up code, whereas last time each constructor would have had to know about the clean-up itself.

You may also have noticed that even the lone `try/catch` we had to include in the first version of this class has now been eliminated—that is, we've written a fully exception-safe and exception-neutral generic container without writing a single `try`! (Who says writing exception-safe code is `trying`?)

Item 14: Writing Exception-Safe Code—Part 7 Difficulty: 5

Only a slight variant—of course, `operator=()` is still very nifty.

Imagine that the `/*????*/` comment in `StackImpl` stood for `public`. Implement all the member functions of the following version of `Stack`, which is to be implemented in terms of `StackImpl` by using a `StackImpl` member object.

```
template <class T>
class Stack
{
public:
  Stack(size_t size=0);
  ~Stack();
  Stack(const Stack&);
  Stack& operator=(const Stack&);
  size_t Count() const;
  void   Push(const T&);
  T&     Top();    // if empty, throws exception
  void   Pop();    // if empty, throws exception
private:
  StackImpl<T> impl_;  // private implementation
};
```

Don't forget exception safety.

Solution

This implementation of `Stack` is only slightly different from the last. For example, `Count()` returns `impl_.vused_` instead of just an inherited `vused_`.

Here's the complete code:

```
template <class T>
class Stack
{
public:
```

```
Stack(size_t size=0)
  : impl_(size)
{
}

Stack(const Stack& other)
  : impl_(other.impl_.vused_)
{
  while( impl_.vused_ < other.impl_.vused_ )
  {
    construct( impl_.v_+impl_.vused_,
               other.impl_.v_[impl_.vused_] );
    ++impl_.vused_;
  }
}

Stack& operator=(const Stack& other)
{
  Stack temp(other);
  impl_.Swap(temp.impl_); // this can't throw
  return *this;
}

size_t Count() const
{
  return impl_.vused_;
}

void Push( const T& t )
{
  if( impl_.vused_ == impl_.vsize_ )
  {
    Stack temp( impl_.vsize_*2+1 );
    while( temp.Count() < impl_.vused_ )
    {
      temp.Push( impl_.v_[temp.Count()] );
    }
    temp.Push( t );
    impl_.Swap( temp.impl_ );
  }
  else
  {
    construct( impl_.v_+impl_.vused_, t );
    ++impl_.vused_;
  }
}

T& Top()
{
  if( impl_.vused_ == 0 )
  {
    throw "empty stack";
  }
  return impl_.v_[impl_.vused_-1];
}
```

```
    void Pop()
    {
      if( impl_.vused_ == 0 )
      {
        throw "pop from empty stack";
      }
      else
      {
        --impl_.vused_;
        destroy( impl_.v_+impl_.vused_ );
      }
    }

  private:
    StackImpl<T> impl_; // private implementation
  };
```

Whew. That's a lot of `impl_`'s. Which brings us to the final question in this miniseries.

Item 15: Writing Exception-Safe Code—Part 8 Difficulty: 9

That's it—this is the final leg of the miniseries. The end of the line is a good place to stop and reflect, and that's just what we'll do for these last three problems.

1. Which technique is better—using `StackImpl` as a private base class, or as a member object?
2. How reusable are the last two versions of `Stack`? What requirements do they put on `T`, the contained type? (In other words, what kinds of `T` can our latest `Stack` accept? The fewer the requirements are, the more reusable `Stack` will be.)
3. Should `Stack` provide exception specifications on its functions?

Solution

Let's answer the questions one at a time.

1. Which technique is better—using `StackImpl` as a private base class, or as a member object?

Both methods give essentially the same effect and nicely separate the two concerns of memory management and object construction/destruction.

When deciding between private inheritance and containment, my rule of thumb is always to prefer the latter and use inheritance only when absolutely necessary. Both techniques mean "is implemented in terms of," and containment forces a better separation of concerns because the using class is a normal client with access to only the used class's public interface. Use private inheritance instead of containment only when absolutely necessary, which means when:

- You need access to the class's protected members, or
- You need to override a virtual function, or
- The object needs to be constructed before other base subobjects[10]

2. How reusable are the last two versions of `Stack`? What requirements do they put on `T`, the contained type?

When writing a templated class, particularly something as potentially widely useful as a generic container, always ask yourself one crucial question: How reusable is my class? Or, to put it a different way: What constraints have I put upon users of the class, and do those constraints unduly limit what those users might want to reasonably do with my class?

These `Stack` templates have two major differences from the first one we built. We've discussed one of the differences already. These latest `Stacks` decouple memory management from contained object construction and destruction, which is nice, but doesn't really affect users. However, there is another important difference. The new `Stacks` construct and destroy individual objects in place as needed, instead of creating default `T` objects in the entire buffer and then assigning them as needed.

This second difference turns out to have significant benefits: better efficiency and reduced requirements on `T`, the contained type. Recall that our original `Stack` required `T` to provide four operations:

- Default constructor (to construct the `v_` buffers)
- Copy constructor (if `Pop` returns by value)
- Nonthrowing destructor (to be able to guarantee exception safety)
- *Exception-safe* copy assignment (To set the values in `v_`, and if the copy assignment throws, then it must guarantee that the target object is still a valid `T`. Note that this is the only `T` member function that must be exception-safe in order for our `Stack` to be exception-safe.)

Now, however, no default construction is needed, because the only `T` construction that's ever performed is copy construction. Further, no copy assignment is needed, because `T` objects are never assigned within `Stack` or `StackImpl`. On the other hand, we now always need a copy constructor. This means that the new `Stacks` require only two things of `T`:

- Copy constructor
- Nonthrowing destructor (to be able to guarantee exception safety)

How does this measure up to our original question about usability? Well, while it's true that many classes have both default constructors and copy assignment operators, many useful classes do not. (In fact, some objects simply cannot be assigned to, such as objects

10. Admittedly, in this case it's tempting to use private inheritance anyway for syntactic convenience so that we don't have to write "`impl_.`" in so many places.

that contain reference members, because they cannot be reseated.) Now even these can be put into `Stacks`, whereas in the original version they could not. That's definitely a big advantage over the original version, and one that quite a few users are likely to appreciate as `Stack` gets reused over time.

Guideline

Design with reuse in mind.

3. Should `Stack` provide exception specifications on its functions?

In short: No, because we, the authors of `Stack`, don't know enough, and we still probably wouldn't want to even if we did know enough. The same is true in principle for any generic container.

First, consider what we, as the authors of `Stack`, do know about `T`, the contained type: precious little. In particular, we don't know in advance which `T` operations might throw or what they might throw. We could always get a little totalitarian about it and start dictating additional requirements on `T`, which would certainly let us know more about `T` and maybe add some useful exception specifications to `Stack`'s member functions. However, doing that would run completely counter to the goal of making `Stack` widely reusable, and so it's really out of the question.

Next, you might notice that some container operations (for example, `Count()`) simply return a scalar value and are known not to throw. Isn't it possible to declare these as `throw()`? Yes, but there are two good reasons why you probably wouldn't.

- Writing `throw()` limits you in the future in case you want to change the underlying implementation to a form that could throw. Loosening an exception specification always runs some risk of breaking existing clients (because the new revision of the class breaks an old promise), so your class will be inherently more resistant to change and therefore more brittle. (Writing `throw()` on virtual functions can also make classes less extensible, because it greatly restricts people who might want to derive from your classes. It can make sense, but such a decision requires careful thought.)
- Exception specifications can incur a performance overhead whether an exception is thrown or not, although many compilers are getting better at minimizing this. For widely-used operations and general-purpose containers, it may be better not to use exception specifications in order to avoid this overhead.

Item 16: Writing Exception-Safe Code—Part 9 Difficulty: 8

How well do you understand the innocuous expression `delete[] p`? What are its implications when it comes to exception safety?

And now, for the topic you've been waiting for: "Destructors That Throw and Why They're Evil."

Consider the expression `delete[] p;`, where `p` points to a valid array on the free store, which was properly allocated and initialized using `new[]`.

1. What does `delete[] p;` really do?
2. How safe is it? Be as specific as possible.

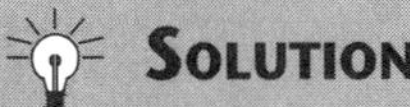

Solution

This brings us to a key topic, namely the innocent looking `delete[] p;`. What does it really do? And how safe is it?

Destructors That Throw and Why They're Evil

First, recall our standard `destroy` helper function (see the accompanying box):

```
template <class FwdIter>
void destroy( FwdIter first, FwdIter last )
{
  while( first != last )
  {
    destroy( &*first ); // calls "*first"'s destructor
    ++first;
  }
}
```

This was safe in our example above, because we required that `T` destructors never throw. But what if a contained object's destructor were allowed to throw? Consider what happens if `destroy` is passed a range of five objects. If the first destructor throws, then as it is written now, `destroy` will exit and the other four objects will never be destroyed. This is obviously not a good thing.

"Ah," you might interrupt, "but can't we clearly get around that by writing `destroy` to work properly in the face of `T`'s whose destructors are allowed to throw?" Well, that's not as clear as one might think. For example, you'd probably start writing something like this:

```
template <class FwdIter>
void destroy( FwdIter first, FwdIter last )
```

```
{
  while( first != last )
  {
    try
    {
      destroy( &*first );
    }
    catch(...)
    {
      /* what goes here? */
    }
    ++first;
  }
}
```

The tricky part is the "what goes here?" There are really only three choices: the catch body rethrows the exception, it converts the exception by throwing something else, or it throws nothing and continues the loop.

1. If the catch body rethrows the exception, then the destroy function nicely meets the requirement of being exception-neutral, because it does indeed allow any T exceptions to propagate out normally. However, it still doesn't meet the safety requirement that no resources be leaked if exceptions occur. Because destroy has no way of signaling how many objects were not successfully destroyed, those objects can never be properly destroyed, so any resources associated with them will be unavoidably leaked. Definitely not good.

2. If the catch body converts the exception by throwing something else, we've clearly failed to meet both the neutrality and the safety requirements. Enough said.

3. If the catch body does not throw or rethrow anything, then the destroy function nicely meets the safety requirement that no resources be leaked if an exception is thrown.[11] However, it obviously fails to meet the neutrality requirement that T exceptions be allowed to pass through because exceptions are absorbed and ignored (as far as the caller is concerned, even if the catch body does attempt to do some sort of logging).

I've seen people suggest that the function should catch the exception and "save" it while continuing to destroy everything else, then rethrow it at the end. That too isn't a solution—for example, it can't correctly deal with multiple exceptions should multiple T destructors throw (even if you save them all until the end, you can end by throwing only one of them and the others are silently absorbed). You might be thinking of other alternatives, but trust me, they all boil down to writing code like this somewhere, because you have a set of objects and they all need to be destroyed. Someone, somewhere, is going to end up writing exception-unsafe code (at best) if T destructors are ever allowed to throw.

---

11. True, if a T destructor could throw in a way that its resources might not be completely released, then there could still be a leak. However, this isn't destroy's problem...this just means that T itself is not exception-safe. But destroy is still properly leak-free in that it doesn't fail to release any resources that it should (namely the T objects themselves).

Which brings us to the innocent-looking `new[]` and `delete[]`.

The issue with both of these is that they have fundamentally the same problem we just described for `destroy`. For example, consider the following code:

```
T* p = new T[10];
delete[] p;
```

Looks like normal, harmless C++, doesn't it? But have you ever wondered what `new[]` and `delete[]` do if a `T` destructor throws? Even if you have wondered, you can't know the answer for the simple reason that there is none. The standard says you get undefined behavior if a `T` destructor throws anywhere in this code, which means that any code that allocates or deallocates an array of objects whose destructors could throw can result in undefined behavior. This may raise some eyebrows, so let's see why this is so.

First, consider what happens if the constructions all succeed and, then, during the `delete[]` operation, the fifth `T` destructor throws. Then `delete[]`, has the same catch-22 problem[12] outlined above for `destroy`. It can't allow the exception to propagate because then the remaining `T` objects would be irretrievably undestroyable, but it also can't translate or absorb the exception because then it wouldn't be exception-neutral.

Second, consider what happens if the fifth constructor throws. Then the fourth object's destructor is invoked, then the third's, and so on until all the `T` objects that were successfully constructed have again been destroyed, and the memory is safely deallocated. But what if things don't go so smoothly? In particular, what if, after the fifth constructor throws, the fourth object's destructor throws? And, if that's ignored, the third's? You can see where this is going.

If destructors may throw, then neither `new[]` nor `delete[]` can be made exception-safe and exception-neutral.

The bottom line is simply this: *Don't ever write destructors that can allow an exception to escape.*[13] If you do write a class with such a destructor, you will not be able to safely even `new[]` or `delete[]` an array of those objects. All destructors should always be implemented as though they had an exception specification of `throw()`—that is, no exceptions must ever be allowed to propagate.

Guideline

Observe the canonical exception safety rules: Never allow an exception to escape from a destructor or from an overloaded `operator delete()` *or* `operator delete[]()`*; write every destructor and deallocation function as though it had an exception specification of "*`throw()`*."*

---

12. Pun intended.

13. As of the London meeting in July of 1997, the draft makes the blanket statement: "No destructor operation defined in the C++ Standard Library will throw an exception." Not only do all the standard classes have this property, but in particular it is not permitted to instantiate a standard container with a type whose destructor does throw. The rest of the guarantees I'm going to outline were fleshed out at the following meeting (Morristown, N.J., November 1997, which was the meeting at which the completed standard was voted out).

Granted, some may feel that this state of affairs is a little unfortunate, because one of the original reasons for having exceptions was to allow both constructors and destructors to report failures (because they have no return values). This isn't quite true, because the intent was mainly for constructor failures (after all, destructors are supposed to destroy, so the scope for failure is definitely less). The good news is that exceptions are still perfectly useful for reporting construction failures, including array and array-`new[]` construction failures, because there they can work predictably, even if a construction does throw.

Safe Exceptions

The advice "be aware, drive with care" certainly applies to writing exception-safe code for containers and other objects. To do it successfully, you do have to meet a sometimes significant extra duty of care. But don't get unduly frightened by exceptions. Apply the guidelines outlined above—that is, isolate your resource management, use the "update a temporary and swap" idiom, and never write classes whose destructors can allow exceptions to escape—and you'll be well on your way to safe and happy production code that is both exception-safe and exception-neutral. The advantages can be both concrete and well worth the trouble for your library and your library's users.

For your convenience (and, hopefully, your future review), here is the "exception safety canonical form" summarized in one place.

> **Guideline**
>
> *Observe the canonical exception-safety rules: (1) Never allow an exception to escape from a destructor or from an overloaded* `operator delete()` *or* `operator delete[]()`*; write every destructor and deallocation function as though it had an exception specification of "*`throw()`*." (2) Always use the "resource acquisition is initialization" idiom to isolate resource ownership and management. (3) In each function, take all the code that might emit an exception and do all that work safely off to the side. Only then, when you know that the real work has succeeded, should you modify the program state (and clean up) using only nonthrowing operations.*

Item 17: Writing Exception-Safe Code—Part 10 Difficulty: 9½

The end—at last. Thank you for considering this miniseries. I hope you've enjoyed it.

At this point, you're probably feeling a little drained and more than a little tired. That's understandable. So here's a final question as a parting gift—it's designed to make everyone remember the equally (if not more) tired people who had to figure this stuff out on their own from first principles and then scrambled hard to get reasonable exception-safety guarantees put into the standard library at the last minute. It's appropriate at this time to repeat public thanks to Dave Abrahams, Greg Colvin, Matt Austern, and all the other "exceptional" people who helped get the current safety guarantees into the standard library—and who managed to complete the job literally days before the standard was frozen in November 1997, at the ISO WG21 / ANSI J16 meeting at Morristown, N.J., USA.

Is the C++ standard library exception-safe?

Explain.

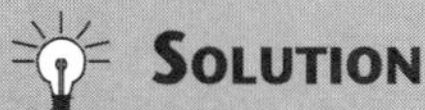

Exception Safety and the Standard Library

Are the standard library containers exception-safe and exception-neutral? The short answer is: Yes.[14]

- All iterators returned from standard containers are exception-safe and can be copied without throwing an exception.
- All standard containers must implement the basic guarantee for all operations: They are always destructible, and they are always in a consistent (if not predictable) state even in the presence of exceptions.
- To make this possible, certain important functions are required to implement the nothrow guarantee (are required not to throw)—including `swap` (the importance of which was illustrated by the example in the previous Item), `allocator<T>::deallocate` (the importance of which was illustrated by the discussion of `operator delete()` at the beginning of this miniseries) and certain operations of the template parameter types themselves (especially, the destructor, the importance of which was illustrated in Item 16 by the discussion headed "Destructors That Throw and Why They're Evil").
- All standard containers must also implement the strong guarantee for all operations (with two exceptions). They always have commit-or-rollback semantics so that an operation such as an `insert` either succeeds completely or else does not change the program state at all. "No change" also means that failed operations do not affect the validity of any iterators that happened to be already pointing into the container.

  There are only two exceptions to this point. First, for all containers, multi-element inserts ("iterator range" inserts) are never strongly exception-safe. Second, for `vector<T>` and `deque<T>` only, inserts and erases (whether single- or multi-element) are strongly exception-safe as long as `T`'s copy constructor and assignment operator do not throw. Note the consequences of these particular limitations. Unfortunately, among other things, this

14. Here, I'm focusing my attention on the containers and iterators portion of the standard library. Other parts of the library, such as iostreams and facets, are specified to provide at least the basic exception-safety guarantee.

means that inserting into and erasing from a `vector<string>` or a `vector<vector<int> >`, for example, are not strongly exception-safe.

Why these particular limitations? Because to roll back either kind of operation isn't possible without extra space/time overhead, and the standard did not want to require that overhead in the name of exception safety. All other container operations can be made strongly exception-safe without overhead. So if you ever insert a range of elements into a container, or if `T`'s copy constructor or assignment operator can throw and you insert into or erase from a `vector<T>` or a `deque<T>`, the container will not necessarily have predictable contents afterward and iterators into it may have been invalidated.

What does this mean for you? Well, if you write a class that has a container member and you perform range insertions, or you write a class that has a member of type `vector<T>` or `deque<T>`, and `T`'s copy constructor or assignment operator can throw, then you are responsible for doing the extra work to ensure that your own class's state is predictable if exceptions do occur. Fortunately, this "extra work" is pretty simple. Whenever you want to insert into or erase from the container, first take a copy of the container, then perform the change on the copy. Finally, use `swap` to switch over to using that new version after you know that the copy-and-change steps have succeeded.

Item 18: Code Complexity—Part 1 — Difficulty: 9

This problem presents an interesting challenge: How many execution paths can there be in a simple three-line function? The answer will almost certainly surprise you.

How many execution paths could there be in the following code?

```
String EvaluateSalaryAndReturnName( Employee e )
{
  if( e.Title() == "CEO" || e.Salary() > 100000 )
  {
    cout << e.First() << " " << e.Last() << " is overpaid" << endl;
  }
  return e.First() + " " + e.Last();
}
```

To provide a little structure here, you should start by relying on the following three assumptions, and then try to expand on them.

1. Different orders of evaluating function parameters are ignored, and failed destructors are ignored.
2. Called functions are considered atomic.
3. To count as a different execution path, an execution path must be made up of a unique sequence of function calls performed and exited in the same way.

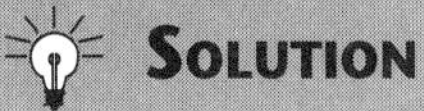

Solution

First, let's think about the implications of the given assumptions:

1. Different orders of evaluating function parameters are ignored, and exceptions thrown by destructors are ignored.[15] Follow-up question for the intrepid: How many more execution paths are there if destructors are allowed to throw?
2. Called functions are considered atomic. For example, the call "`e.Title()`" could throw for several reasons (for example, it could throw an exception itself, it could fail to catch an exception thrown by another function it has called, or it could return by value and the temporary object's constructor could throw). All that matters to the function is whether performing the operation `e.Title()` results in an exception being thrown or not.
3. To count as a different execution path, an execution path must be made up of a unique sequence of function calls performed and exited in the same way.

So, how many possible execution paths are there? Answer: *23* (in just three lines of code!).

If you found:	*Rate yourself:*
3	Average
4–14	Exception-aware
15–23	Guru material

The 23 are made up of:

- 3 nonexceptional code paths
- 20 invisible exceptional code paths

By *nonexceptional code paths* I mean paths of execution that happen even if there are no exceptions thrown. Nonexceptional code paths result from normal C++ program flow. On the other hand, by *exceptional code paths* I mean those paths of execution that arise as a result of an exception being thrown or propagated, and I'll consider those paths separately.

Nonexceptional Code Paths

For the nonexceptional execution paths, the trick was to know C/C++'s short-circuit evaluation rule.

```
if( e.Title() == "CEO" || e.Salary() > 100000 )
```

1. If `e.Title() == "CEO"` evaluates to `true`, then the second part of the condition doesn't need to be evaluated (for example, `e.Salary()` will never be called), but the `cout` will be performed.

15. Never allow an exception to propagate from a destructor. Code that does this can't be made to work well. See Item 16 for more about "destructors that throw and why they're evil."

With suitable overloads for ==, ||, and/or > in the if's condition, the || could actually turn out to be a function call. If it is a function call, the short-circuit evaluation rule would be suppressed and both parts of the condition would be evaluated all the time.

2. If `e.Title() != "CEO"` but `e.Salary() > 100000`, both parts of the condition will be evaluated and the `cout` will be performed.

3. If `e.Title() != "CEO"` and `e.Salary() <= 100000`, the `cout` will not be performed.

Exceptional Code Paths

This leaves the exceptional execution paths.

```
String EvaluateSalaryAndReturnName( Employee e )
  ^*^                                  ^4^
```

4. The argument is passed by value, which invokes the `Employee` copy constructor. This copy operation might throw an exception.

*. `String`'s copy constructor might throw while copying the temporary return value into the caller's area. We'll ignore this one, however, because it happens outside this function (and it turns out that we have enough execution paths of our own to keep us busy anyway).

```
if( e.Title() == "CEO" || e.Salary() > 100000 )
       ^5^    ^7^  ^6^ ^11^    ^8^    ^10^  ^9^
```

5. The `Title()` member function might itself throw, or it might return an object of class type by value, and that copy operation might throw.

6. To match a valid `operator==()`, the string literal may need to be converted to a temporary object of class type (probably the same as `e.Title()`'s return type), and that construction of the temporary might throw.

7. If `operator==()` is a programmer-supplied function, it might throw.

8. Similar to #5, `Salary()` might itself throw, or it might return a temporary object and this construction operation might throw.

9. Similar to #6, a temporary object may need to be constructed and this construction might throw.

10. Similar to #7, this might be a programmer-provided function and therefore might throw.

11. Similar to #7 and #10, this might be a programmer-provided function and therefore might throw.

```
cout << e.First() << " " << e.Last() << " is overpaid" << endl;
    ^12^ ^17^    ^13^    ^14^  ^18^  ^15^              ^16^
```

12–16. As documented in the C++ Standard, any of the five calls to `operator<<` might throw.

17–18. Similar to #5, `First()` and/or `Last()` might throw, or each might return a temporary object and those construction operations might throw.

```
return e.First()   +    " "   +   e.Last();
       ^19^      ^22^ ^21^ ^23^   ^20^
```

19–20. Similar to #5, `First()` and/or `Last()` might throw, or each might return a temporary object and those construction operations might throw.

21. Similar to #6, a temporary object may need to be constructed and this construction might throw.

22–23. Similar to #7, this might be a programmer-provided function and therefore might throw.

Guideline

Always be exception-aware. Know what code might emit exceptions.

One purpose of this Item was to demonstrate just how many invisible execution paths can exist in simple code in a language that allows exceptions. Does this invisible complexity affect the function's reliability and testability? See the following Item for the answer.

Item 19: Code Complexity—Part 2 — Difficulty: 7

The challenge: Take the three-line function from Item 18 and make it exception-safe. This exercise illustrates some important lessons about exception safety.

Is the function from Item 18 exception-safe (works properly in the presence of exceptions) and exception-neutral (propagates all exceptions to the caller)?

```
String EvaluateSalaryAndReturnName( Employee e )
{
  if( e.Title() == "CEO" || e.Salary() > 100000 )
  {
    cout << e.First() << " " << e.Last() << " is overpaid" << endl;
  }
  return e.First() + " " + e.Last();
}
```

Explain your answer. If it is exception-safe, does it support the basic guarantee, the strong guarantee, or the nothrow guarantee? If not, how must it be changed to support one of these guarantees?

Assume that all called functions are strongly exception-safe (might throw but do not have side effects), and that any objects being used, including temporaries, are exception-safe (clean up their resources when destroyed).

To recap the basic, strong, and nothrow guarantees, see Item 11. In brief, the basic guarantee ensures destructibility and no leaks; the strong guarantee, in addition, ensures full commit-or-rollback semantics; and the nothrow guarantee ensures that a function will not emit an exception.

Solution

First, before we get into the solution proper, a word about assumptions.

As the problem stated, we will assume that all called functions—including the stream functions—are strongly exception-safe (might throw but do not have side effects), and that any objects being used, including temporaries, are exception-safe (clean up their resources when destroyed).

Streams happen to throw a monkey wrench into this because of their possible "un-rollbackable" side effects. For example, `operator<<` might throw after emitting part of a string that can't be "un-emitted"; also, the stream's error state may be set. We will ignore those issues for the most part; the point of this discussion is to examine how to make a function exception-safe when the function is specified to have two distinct side effects.

So here's the question again: Is the function from Item 18 exception-safe (works properly in the presence of exceptions) and exception-neutral (propagates all exceptions to the caller)?

```
String EvaluateSalaryAndReturnName( Employee e )
{
  if( e.Title() == "CEO" || e.Salary() > 100000 )
  {
    cout << e.First() << " " << e.Last() << " is overpaid" << endl;
  }
  return e.First() + " " + e.Last();
}
```

As written, this function satisfies the basic guarantee: In the presence of exceptions, the function does not leak resources.

This function does *not* satisfy the strong guarantee. The strong guarantee says that if the function fails due to an exception, program state must not be changed. `EvaluateSalaryAndReturnName()`, however, has two distinct side effects (as hinted at in the function's name).

- An "`...overpaid...`" message is emitted to `cout`.
- A name string is returned.

As far as the second side effect is concerned, the function already meets the strong guarantee, because if an exception occurs the value will never be returned. As far as the first side effect is concerned, though, the function is not exception-safe for two reasons:

- If an exception is thrown after the first part of the message has been emitted to `cout` but before the message has been completed (for example, if the fourth `operator<<` throws), then a partial message was emitted to `cout`.[16]
- If the message was emitted successfully but an exception occurs later in the function (for example, during the assembly of the return value), then a message was emitted to `cout` even though the function failed because of an exception.

Finally, the function clearly does not satisfy the nothrow guarantee: Lots of operations might throw, and there's no `try/catch` block or `throw()` specification in sight.

Guideline

Understand the basic, strong, and nothrow exception-safety guarantees.

To meet the strong guarantee, either both effects are completed or an exception is thrown and neither effect is performed.

Can we accomplish this? Here's one way we might try it:

```
// Attempt #1: An improvement?
//
String EvaluateSalaryAndReturnName( Employee e )
{
  String result = e.First() + " " + e.Last();

  if( e.Title() == "CEO" || e.Salary() > 100000 )
  {
    String message = result + " is overpaid\n";
    cout << message;
  }

  return result;
}
```

This isn't bad. Note that we've replaced the `endl` with a newline character (which isn't exactly equivalent) in order to get the entire string into one `operator<<` call. (Of course, this doesn't guarantee that the underlying stream system won't itself fail partway through writing the message, resulting in incomplete output, but at least we've done the best we can do at this high level.)

---

16. If you're thinking that it's a little pedantic to worry about whether a message is completely `cout`'ed or not, you're partly right. In this case, maybe no one would care. However, the same principle applies to any function that attempts to perform two side effects, and that's why the following discussion is useful.

We still have one minor quibble, however, as illustrated by the following client code:

```
// A problem...
//
String theName;
theName = EvaluateSalaryAndReturnName( bob );
```

The `String` copy constructor is invoked because the result is returned by value, and the copy assignment operator is invoked to copy the result into `theName`. If either copy fails, then the function has completed its side effects (since the message was completely emitted and the return value was completely constructed), but the result has been irretrievably lost (oops).

Can we do better, and perhaps avoid the problem by avoiding the copy? For example, we could let the function take a non-`const` `String` reference parameter and place the return value in that.

```
// Attempt #2: Better now?
//
void EvaluateSalaryAndReturnName( Employee e,
                                  String&  r )
{
  String result = e.First() + " " + e.Last();

  if( e.Title() == "CEO" || e.Salary() > 100000 )
  {
    String message = result + " is overpaid\n";
    cout << message;
  }

  r = result;
}
```

This may look better, but it isn't, because the assignment to `r` might still fail, which leaves us with one side effect complete and the other incomplete. Bottom line, this attempt doesn't really buy us much.

One way to solve the problem is to return a pointer to a dynamically allocated `String`. But the best solution is to go a step farther and return the pointer in an `auto_ptr`.

```
// Attempt #3: Correct (finally!).
//
auto_ptr<String>
EvaluateSalaryAndReturnName( Employee e )
{
  auto_ptr<String> result
      = new String( e.First() + " " + e.Last() );

  if( e.Title() == "CEO" || e.Salary() > 100000 )
  {
    String message = (*result) + " is overpaid\n";
    cout << message;
  }

  return result;  // rely on transfer of ownership;
                  // this can't throw
}
```

This does the trick, because we have effectively hidden all the work to construct the second side effect (the return value), while we ensured that it can be safely returned to the caller using only nonthrowing operations after the first side effect has completed (the printing of the message). We know that once the function is complete, the returned value will make it successfully into the hands of the caller and be correctly cleaned up in all cases. If the caller accepts the returned value, the act of accepting a copy of the `auto_ptr` causes the caller to take ownership; and if the caller does not accept the returned value, say by ignoring the return value, the allocated `String` will automatically be cleaned up as the temporary `auto_ptr` holding it is destroyed. The price for this extra safety? As often happens when implementing strong exception safety, the strong safety comes at the (usually minor) cost of some efficiency—here, the extra dynamic memory allocation. But, when it comes to trading off efficiency for predictability and correctness, we ought to prefer the latter two.

Let's discuss, for a moment, exception safety and multiple side effects. In this case, it turned out to be possible in Attempt #3 to perform both side effects with essentially commit-or-rollback semantics (except for the stream issues). It was possible because there turned out to be a technique by which the two effects could be performed atomically—that is, all the "real" preparatory work for both could be completed in such a way that actually performing the visible side effects could be done using only nonthrowing operations.

Even though we were lucky this time, it's not always that simple. It's impossible to write strongly exception-safe functions that have two or more unrelated side effects that cannot be performed atomically (for example, what if the two side effects here had been to emit one message to `cout` and another to `cerr`?), since the strong guarantee states that in the presence of exceptions "program state will remain unchanged"—in other words, if there's an exception, there must be *no* side effects. When you come across a case in which the two side effects cannot be made to work atomically, usually the only way to get strong exception safety is to split the one function into two others that can be performed atomically. That way, at least, the fact that they can't be done atomically is visible to the calling code.

Guideline

Prefer cohesion. Always endeavor to give each piece of code—each module, each class, each function—a single, well-defined responsibility.

In summary, this Item illustrates three important points.

1. Providing the strong exception-safety guarantee often (but not always) requires you to trade off performance.
2. If a function has multiple unrelated side effects, it cannot always be made strongly exception-safe. If not, it can be done only by splitting the function into several functions, each of whose side effects can be performed atomically.
3. Not all functions need to be strongly exception-safe. Both the original code and Attempt #1 satisfy the basic guarantee. For many clients, Attempt #1 is sufficient and minimizes the opportunity for side effects to occur in the exceptional situations, without requiring the performance tradeoffs of Attempt #3.

There's a postscript to this solution regarding streams and side effects.

In this Item's problem statement, I said in part: Assume that all called functions are exception-safe (might throw but do not have side effects if they do throw), and that any objects being used, including temporaries, are exception-safe (clean up their resources when destroyed).

As it turns out, our assumption that no called function has side effects cannot be entirely true. In particular, there is no way to guarantee that the stream operations will not fail after partly emitting a result. This means that we can't get true commit-or-rollback fidelity from any function that performs stream output, at least not on these standard streams.

Another issue is that if the stream output fails, the stream state will have changed. We currently do not check for that or recover from it, but it is possible to further refine the function to catch stream exceptions and reset `cout`'s error flags before rethrowing the exception to the caller.

Class Design and Inheritance

Item 20: Class Mechanics — Difficulty: 7

How good are you at the details of writing classes? This item focuses not only on blatant errors, but even more so on professional style. Understanding these principles will help you to design classes that are more robust and easier to maintain.

You are doing a code review. A programmer has written the following class, which shows some poor style and has some real errors. How many can you find, and how would you fix them?

```
class Complex
{
public:
  Complex( double real, double imaginary = 0 )
    : _real(real), _imaginary(imaginary)
  {
  }
  void operator+ ( Complex other )
  {
    _real = _real + other._real;
    _imaginary = _imaginary + other._imaginary;
  }
  void operator<<( ostream os )
  {
    os << "(" << _real << "," << _imaginary << ")";
  }
  Complex operator++()
  {
    ++_real;
    return *this;
  }
  Complex operator++( int )
```

```
    {
      Complex temp = *this;
      ++_real;
      return temp;
    }
  private:
    double _real, _imaginary;
  };
```

Solution

This class has a lot of problems—even more than I will explicitly show here. The point of this puzzle is primarily to highlight class mechanics (issues such as "what is the canonical form of `operator<<`?" and "should `operator+` be a member?") rather than point out where the interface is just plain poorly designed. However, I will start off with perhaps the most useful observation: Why write a `Complex` class when one already exists in the standard library? And, what's more, the standard one isn't plagued with any of the following problems and has been crafted based on years of practice by the best people in our industry. Humble thyself and reuse.

> **Guideline**
>
> *Reuse code—especially standard library code—instead of handcrafting your own. It's faster, easier, and safer.*

Perhaps the best way to fix the problems in the `Complex` code is to avoid using the class at all and use the `std::complex` template instead.

Having said that, let's go through the class as written and fix the problems as we go. First, the constructor:

1. The constructor allows an implicit conversion.

```
Complex( double real, double imaginary = 0 )
  : _real(real), _imaginary(imaginary)
{
}
```

Because the second parameter has a default value, this function can be used as a single-parameter constructor and, hence, as an implicit conversion from `double` to `Complex`. In this case, it's probably fine, but as we saw in Item 6, the conversion may not always be intended. In general it's a good idea to make your constructors explicit by default unless you deliberately decide to allow the implicit conversion. (See Item 39 for more about implicit conversions.)

Guideline

Watch out for hidden temporaries created by implicit conversions. One good way to avoid this is to make constructors `explicit` *when possible, and avoid writing conversion operators.*

2. `operator+` is probably slightly inefficient.

```
void operator+ ( Complex other )
{
  _real = _real + other._real;
  _imaginary = _imaginary + other._imaginary;
}
```

For efficiency, the parameter should be passed by reference to `const`.

Guideline

Prefer passing objects by `const&` *instead of passing by value.*

Also, in both cases, "a=a+b" should be rewritten "a+=b". Doing that won't give you great efficiency gains in this particular case because we're only adding `double`s, but it can make a significant difference with class types.

Guideline

Prefer writing "`a op= b;`*" instead of "*`a = a op b;`*" (where* `op` *stands for any operator). It's clearer, and it's often more efficient.*

The reason why `operator+=` is more efficient is that it operates on the left-hand object directly and returns only a reference, not a temporary object. On the other hand, `operator+` must return a temporary object. To see why, consider the following canonical forms for how `operator+=` and `operator+` should normally be implemented for some type `T`.

```
T& T::operator+=( const T& other )
{
  //...
  return *this;
}

const T operator+( const T& a, const T& b )
{
  T temp( a );
  temp += b;
  return temp;
}
```

Notice the relationship between operators + and +=. The former should be implemented in terms of the latter, both for simplicity (the code is easier to write) and for consistency (the two will do the same thing and are less likely to diverge during maintenance).

> **Guideline**
>
> *If you supply a standalone version of an operator (for example,* `operator+`*), always supply an assignment version of the same operator (for example,* `operator+=`*) and prefer implementing the former in terms of the latter. Also, always preserve the natural relationship between* `op` *and* `op=` *(where* `op` *stands for any operator).*

3. `operator+` should not be a member function.

```
void operator+ ( Complex other )
{
  _real = _real + other._real;
  _imaginary = _imaginary + other._imaginary;
}
```

If `operator+` is made a member function, as it is here, then it won't work as naturally as your users may expect when you do decide to allow implicit conversions from other types. Specifically, when adding `Complex` objects to numeric values, you can write "`a = b + 1.0`" but not "`a = 1.0 + b`" because a member `operator+` requires a `Complex` (and not a `const double`) as its left-hand argument.

Also, if do you want your users to be able to add `Complex` objects to `double`s conveniently, it may make sense to provide the overloaded functions `operator+(const Complex&, double)` and `operator+(double, const Complex&)` too.

> **Guideline**
>
> *The standard requires that operators* `=` `()` `[]` *and* `->` *must be members, and class-specific operators* `new`*,* `new[]`*,* `delete`*, and* `delete[]` *must be static members. For all other functions:*
>
> *if the function is* `operator>>` *or* `operator<<` *for stream I/O,*
> *or if it needs type conversions on its leftmost argument,*
> *or if it can be implemented using the class's public interface alone,*
>   *make it a nonmember (and friend if needed in the first two cases)*
>   *if it needs to behave virtually,*
>   *add a virtual member function to provide the virtual behavior,*
>   *and implement it in terms of that*
> *else*
>   *make it a member*

4. `operator+` should not modify this object's value, and it should return a temporary object containing the sum.

```
void operator+ ( Complex other )
{
  _real = _real + other._real;
  _imaginary = _imaginary + other._imaginary;
}
```

Note that the return type for the temporary should be "const Complex" (not just "Complex") in order to prevent usage like "a+b=c".

5. You should normally define op= if you define op. Here, you should define operator+=, since you defined operator+, and then implement the latter in terms of the former.

6. operator<< should not be a member function.

```
void operator<< ( ostream os )
{
  os << "(" << _real << "," << _imaginary << ")";
}
```

See again the similar discussion above about operator+. Also, the parameters should be "(ostream&, const Complex&)". Note that the nonmember operator<< should normally be implemented in terms of a(n often virtual) member function that does the work, usually named something like Print().

Also, for a real operator<<, you should do things like check the stream's current format flags to conform to common usage. Check your favorite standard library or iostreams book for details.

7. Further, operator<< should have a return type of "ostream&" and should return a reference to the stream in order to permit chaining. That way, users can use your operator<< naturally in code like "cout << a << b;".

Guideline

Always return stream references from operator<< *and* operator>>.

8. The preincrement operator's return type is incorrect.

```
Complex operator++()
{
  ++_real;
  return *this;
}
```

Preincrement should return a reference to non-const—in this case, Complex&. This lets client code operate more intuitively and avoids needless inefficiency.

9. The postincrement operator's return type is incorrect.

```
Complex operator++( int )
{
  Complex temp = *this;
  ++_real;
  return temp;
}
```

Postincrement should return a const value—in this case, const Complex. By not allowing changes to the returned object, we prevent questionable code like "a++++", which doesn't do what a naïve user might think it does.

10. Postincrement should be implemented in terms of preincrement. See Item 6 for the canonical form for postincrement.

> **Guideline**
>
> *For consistency, always implement postincrement in terms of preincrement. Otherwise, your users will get surprising (and often unpleasant) results.*

11. Avoid reserved names.

```
private:
  double _real, _imaginary;
```

Yes, popular books like *Design Patterns* (Gamma95) do use leading underscores in variable names, but don't do it. The standard reserves some leading-underscore identifiers for the implementation, and the rules are hard enough to remember—for you and for compiler writers—that you may as well avoid leading underscores entirely.[1] Instead, my own preference is to follow the convention of designating member variable names with a trailing underscore.

That's it. Here's a corrected version of the class, ignoring design and style issues not explicitly noted above:

```
class Complex
{
public:
  explicit Complex( double real, double imaginary = 0 )
    : real_(real), imaginary_(imaginary)
  {
  }

  Complex& operator+=( const Complex& other )
  {
    real_ += other.real_;
    imaginary_ += other.imaginary_;
    return *this;
  }

  Complex& operator++()
  {
    ++real_;
    return *this;
  }
```

1. For example, names with leading underscores are technically reserved only for nonmember names, so some would argue that this isn't a problem and that class member names with leading underscores are fine. That's not entirely true in practice, because some implementations `#define` macros with leading-underscore names, and macros don't respect scope. They'll tromp on your member names as easily as they'll tromp on your nonmember names. It's easier just to leave all leading underscores for implementers and avoid the possible hassles.

```
  const Complex operator++( int )
  {
    Complex temp( *this );
    ++*this;
    return temp;
  }

  ostream& Print( ostream& os ) const
  {
    return os << "(" << real_ << "," << imaginary_ << ")";
  }

private:
  double real_, imaginary_;
};

const Complex operator+( const Complex& lhs, const Complex& rhs )
{
  Complex ret( lhs );
  ret += rhs;
  return ret;
}

ostream& operator<<( ostream& os, const Complex& c )
{
  return c.Print(os);
}
```

Item 21: Overriding Virtual Functions — Difficulty: 6

Virtual functions are a pretty basic feature, but they occasionally harbor subtleties that trap the unwary. If you can answer questions like this one, then you know virtual functions cold, and you're less likely to waste a lot of time debugging problems like the ones illustrated below.

In your travels through the dusty corners of your company's code archives, you come across the following program fragment written by an unknown programmer. The programmer seems to have been experimenting to see how some C++ features work. What did the programmer probably expect the program to print, and what is the actual result?

```
#include <iostream>
#include <complex>
using namespace std;
class Base
{
public:
  virtual void f( int );
  virtual void f( double );
  virtual void g( int i = 10 );
};
```

```
void Base::f( int )
{
  cout << "Base::f(int)" << endl;
}
void Base::f( double )
{
  cout << "Base::f(double)" << endl;
}
void Base::g( int i )
{
  cout << i << endl;
}
class Derived: public Base
{
public:
  void f( complex<double> );
  void g( int i = 20 );
};
void Derived::f( complex<double> )
{
  cout << "Derived::f(complex)" << endl;
}
void Derived::g( int i )
{
  cout << "Derived::g() " << i << endl;
}
void main()
{
  Base    b;
  Derived d;
  Base*   pb = new Derived;
  b.f(1.0);
  d.f(1.0);
  pb->f(1.0);
  b.g();
  d.g();
  pb->g();
  delete pb;
}
```

Solution

First, let's consider some style issues, and one real error.

1. "`void main()`" is nonstandard and therefore nonportable.

```
void main()
```

Yes, alas, I know that this appears in many books. Some authors even argue that "`void main()`" might be standard-conforming. It isn't. It never was, not even in the 1970s, in the original pre-standard C.

Even though "`void main()`" is not one of the legal declarations of `main`, many compilers allow it. What this means, however, is that even if you are able to write "`void main()`" today on your current compiler, you may not be able to write it when you port to a new compiler. It's best to get into the habit of using either of the two standard and portable declarations of `main`:

```
int main()
int main( int argc, char* argv[] )
```

You might also have noticed that the problem program does not have a return statement in `main`. Even with a standard `main()` that returns an `int`, that's not a problem (though it's certainly good style to report errors to outside callers), because if `main()` has no return statement, the effect is that of executing "`return 0;`". Caveat: As of this writing, many compilers still do not implement this rule and will emit warnings if you don't put an explicit `return` statement in `main()`.

2. "`delete pb;`" is unsafe.

```
delete pb;
```

This looks innocuous. It would be innocuous, if only the writer of `Base` had supplied a virtual destructor. As it is, deleting via a pointer-to-base without a virtual destructor is evil, pure and simple, and corruption is the best thing you can hope for, because the wrong destructor will get called and `operator delete()` will be invoked with the wrong object size.

Guideline

Make base class destructors virtual (unless you are certain that no one will ever attempt to delete a derived object through a pointer to base).

For the next few points, it's important to differentiate between three common terms:

- To *overload* a function `f()` means to provide another function with the same name (`f`) in the same scope but with different parameter types. When `f()` is actually called, the compiler will try to pick the best match based on the actual parameters that are supplied.
- To *override* a virtual function `f()` means to provide another function with the same name (`f`) and the same parameter types in a derived class.
- To *hide* a function `f()` in an enclosing scope (base class, outer class, or namespace) means to provide another function with the same name (`f`) in an inner scope (derived class, nested class, or namespace), which will hide the same function name in an enclosing scope.

3. `Derived::f` is not an overload.

```
void Derived::f( complex<double> )
```

`Derived` does not overload `Base::f`, it hides them. This distinction is very important, because it means that `Base::f(int)` and `Base::f(double)` are not visible in the scope of

Derived. (Amazingly, certain popular compilers do not even emit a warning for this, so it's all the more important that you know about it.)

If the author of Derived intended to hide the Base functions named f, then this is all right.[2] Usually, however, the hiding is inadvertent and surprising, and the correct way to bring the names into the scope of Derived is to write the using-declaration "using Base::f;".

Guideline

When providing a function with the same name as an inherited function, be sure to bring the inherited functions into scope with a using-declaration if you don't want to hide them.

4. Derived::g overrides Base::g but changes the default parameter.

```
void g( int i = 20 )
```

This is decidedly user-unfriendly. Unless you're really out to confuse people, don't change the default parameters of the inherited functions you override. (In general, it's not a bad idea to prefer overloading to parameter defaulting anyway, but that's a subject in itself.) Yes, this is legal C++; and yes, the result is well-defined; and no, don't do it.

Further on, we'll see how this can really confuse people.

Guideline

Never change the default parameters of overridden inherited functions.

Now that we have those issues out of the way, let's look at the mainline and see whether it does what the programmer intended.

```
void main()
{
  Base    b;
  Derived d;
  Base*   pb = new Derived;

  b.f(1.0);
```

No problem. This first call invokes Base::f(double), as expected.

```
  d.f(1.0);
```

This calls Derived::f(complex<double>). Why? Well, remember that Derived doesn't declare "using Base::f;" to bring the Base functions named f into scope, and so,

2. When deliberately hiding a base name, it's clearer to do it by writing a private using declaration for the name.

clearly, `Base::f( int )` and `Base::f( double )` can't be called. They are not present in the same scope as `Derived::f( complex<double> )` so as to participate in overloading.

The programmer may have expected this to call `Base::f( double )`, but in this case there won't even be a compile error, because, fortunately(?), `complex<double>` provides an implicit conversion from `double`, so the compiler interprets this call to mean `Derived::f( complex<double>(1.0) )`.

```
    pb->f(1.0);
```

Interestingly, even though the `Base* pb` is pointing to a `Derived` object, this calls `Base::f( double )`, because overload resolution is done on the static type (here `Base`), not the dynamic type (here `Derived`).

For the same reason, the call "`pb->f(complex<double>(1.0));`" would not compile, because there is no satisfactory function in the `Base` interface.

```
    b.g();
```

This prints "`10`", because it simply invokes `Base::g( int )` whose parameter defaults to the value 10. No sweat.

```
    d.g();
```

This prints "`Derived::g() 20`", because it simply invokes `Derived::g( int )` whose parameter defaults to the value 20. Also no sweat.

```
    pb->g();
```

This prints "`Derived::g() 10`".

"Wait a minute," you protest, "what's going on here?" This result may temporarily lock your mental brakes and bring you to a screeching halt until you realize that what the compiler has done is quite proper.[3] The thing to remember is that, like overloads, default parameters are taken from the static type (here `Base`) of the object, hence the default value of 10 is taken. However, the function happens to be virtual, so the function actually called is based on the dynamic type (here `Derived`) of the object.

If you understand the last few paragraphs about name hiding and when static versus dynamic types are used, then you understand this stuff cold. Congratulations!

```
    delete pb;
}
```

Finally, as noted, the delete will of course corrupt your memory anyway and leave things partially destroyed; see the part about virtual destructors above.

3. Although, of course, the programmer of `Derived` ought to be taken out into the back parking lot and yelled at.

Item 22: Class Relationships—Part 1 Difficulty: 5

How are your OO design skills? This Item illustrates a common class design mistake that still catches many programmers.

A networking application has two kinds of communications sessions, each with its own message protocol. The two protocols have similarities (some computations and even some messages are the same), so the programmer has come up with the following design to encapsulate the common computations and messages in a `BasicProtocol` class.

```
class BasicProtocol /* : possible base classes */
{
public:
  BasicProtocol();
  virtual ~BasicProtocol();
  bool BasicMsgA( /*...*/ );
  bool BasicMsgB( /*...*/ );
  bool BasicMsgC( /*...*/ );
};

class Protocol1 : public BasicProtocol
{
public:
  Protocol1();
  ~Protocol1();
  bool DoMsg1( /*...*/ );
  bool DoMsg2( /*...*/ );
  bool DoMsg3( /*...*/ );
  bool DoMsg4( /*...*/ );
};

class Protocol2 : public BasicProtocol
{
public:
  Protocol2();
  ~Protocol2();
  bool DoMsg1( /*...*/ );
  bool DoMsg2( /*...*/ );
  bool DoMsg3( /*...*/ );
  bool DoMsg4( /*...*/ );
  bool DoMsg5( /*...*/ );
};
```

Each `DoMsg...()` member function calls the `BasicProtocol::Basic...()` functions as needed to perform the common work, but the `DoMsg...()` function performs the actual transmissions itself. Each class may have additional members, but you can assume that all significant members are shown.

Comment on this design. Is there anything you would change? If so, why?

Solution

This Item illustrates a too-common pitfall in OO class relationship design. To recap, classes `Protocol1` and `Protocol2` are publicly derived from a common base class `BasicProtocol`, which performs some common work.

A key to identifying the problem is the following:

> *Each `DoMsg...()` member function calls the `BasicProtocol::Basic...()` functions as needed to perform the common work, but the `DoMsg...()` function performs the actual transmissions itself.*

Here we have it: This is clearly describing an "is implemented in terms of" relationship, which, in C++, is spelled either "private inheritance" or "membership." Unfortunately, many people still frequently misspell it as "public inheritance," thereby confusing implementation inheritance with interface inheritance. The two are not the same thing, and that confusion is at the root of the problem here.

Common Mistake

Never use public inheritance except to model true Liskov IS-A and WORKS-LIKE-A. All overridden member functions must require no more and promise no less.

Incidentally, programmers in the habit of making this mistake (using public inheritance for implementation) usually end up creating deep inheritance hierarchies. This greatly increases the maintenance burden by adding unnecessary complexity, forcing users to learn the interfaces of many classes even when all they want to do is use a specific derived class. It can also have an impact on memory use and program performance by adding unnecessary vtables and indirections to classes that do not really need them. If you find yourself frequently creating deep inheritance hierarchies, you should review your design style to see if you've picked up this bad habit. Deep hierarchies are rarely needed and almost never good. And if you don't believe that but think that "OO just isn't OO without lots of inheritance," then a good counter-example to consider is the standard library itself.

Guideline

Never inherit publicly to reuse code (in the base class); inherit publicly in order to be reused (by code that uses base objects polymorphically).[4]

4. I got this guideline from (and use it with thanks to) Marshall Cline, who is co-author of the classic *C++ FAQs* book (Cline 95).

In a little more detail, here are several clues that help indicate this problem.

1. `BasicProtocol` provides no virtual functions (other than the destructor, which we'll get to in a minute).[5] This means that it is not intended to be used polymorphically, which is a strong hint against public inheritance.

2. `BasicProtocol` has no protected functions or members. This means that there is no "derivation interface," which is a strong hint against any inheritance at all, either public or private.

3. `BasicProtocol` encapsulates common work, but as described, it does not seem to actually perform its own transmissions as the derived classes do. This means that a `BasicProtocol` object does not WORK-LIKE-A derived protocol object, nor is it USABLE-AS-A derived protocol object. Public inheritance should be used to model one thing and one thing only—a true interface IS-A relationship that obeys the Liskov Substitution Principle. For greater clarity, I usually call this WORKS-LIKE-A or USABLE-AS-A.[6]

4. The derived classes use `BasicProtocol`'s public interface only. This means that they do not benefit from being derived classes, and could as easily perform their work using a separate helper object of type `BasicProtocol`.

This means we have a few clean-up issues. First, because `BasicProtocol` is clearly not designed to be derived from, its virtual destructor is unnecessary (indeed, misleading) and should be eliminated. Second, `BasicProtocol` should probably be renamed to something less misleading, such as `MessageCreator` or `MessageHelper`.

Once we've made those changes, which option should be used to model this "is implemented in terms of" relationship—private inheritance or membership? The answer is pretty easy to remember.

> **Guideline**
>
> *When modeling "is implemented in terms of," always prefer membership/containment, not inheritance. Use private inheritance only when inheritance is absolutely necessary—that is, when you need access to protected members or you need to override a virtual function. Never use public inheritance for code reuse.*

Using membership forces a better separation of concerns, because the using class is a normal client with access to only the used class's public interface. Prefer it, and you'll find that your code is cleaner, easier to read, and easier to maintain. In short, your code will cost less.

---

5. Even if `BasicProtocol` were itself derived from another class, we come to the same conclusion, because it still does not provide any new virtual functions. If some base class does provide virtual functions, then it's that remote base class that's intended to be used polymorphically, not `BasicProtocol` itself. So, if anything, we should be deriving from that remote base instead.
6. Yes, sometimes, when you inherit publicly to get an interface, some implementation can come along, too, if the base class has both an interface that you want and some implementation of its own. This is nearly always possible to design away (see the next Item), but it's not always necessary to take the true purist approach of "one responsibility per class."

Item 23: Class Relationships—Part 2 Difficulty: 6

Design patterns are an important tool in writing reusable code. Do you recognize the patterns used in this Item? If so, can you improve them?

A database manipulation program often needs to do some work on every record (or selected records) in a given table, by first performing a read-only pass through the table to cache information about which records need to be processed, and then performing a second pass to actually make the changes.

Instead of rewriting much of the common logic each time, a programmer has tried to provide a generic reusable framework in the following abstract class. The intent is that the abstract class should encapsulate the repetitive work by first, compiling a list of table rows on which work needs to be done, and second, by performing the work on each affected row. Derived classes are responsible for providing the details of their specific operations.

```
//----------------------------------------------------
// File gta.h
//----------------------------------------------------
class GenericTableAlgorithm
{
public:
  GenericTableAlgorithm( const string& table );
  virtual ~GenericTableAlgorithm();

  // Process() returns true if and only if successful.
  // It does all the work: a) physically reads
  // the table's records, calling Filter() on each
  // to determine whether it should be included
  // in the rows to be processed; and b) when the
  // list of rows to operate upon is complete, calls
  // ProcessRow() for each such row.
  //
  bool Process();

private:
  // Filter() returns true if and only if the row should be
  // included in the ones to be processed. The
  // default action is to return true (to include
  // every row).
  //
  virtual bool Filter( const Record& );

  // ProcessRow() is called once per record that
  // was included for processing. This is where
  // the concrete class does its specialized work.
  // (Note: This means every row to be processed
  // will be read twice, but assume that that is
  // necessary and not an efficiency consideration.)
  //
  virtual bool ProcessRow( const PrimaryKey& ) =0;
```

```
  struct GenericTableAlgorithmImpl* pimpl_; // MYOB
};
```

For example, the client code to derive a concrete worker class and use it in a mainline looks something like this:

```
class MyAlgorithm : public GenericTableAlgorithm
{
  // ... override Filter() and ProcessRow() to
  //     implement a specific operation ...
};
int main()
{
  MyAlgorithm a( "Customer" );
  a.Process();
}
```

The questions are:

1. This is a good design and implements a well-known design pattern. Which pattern is this? Why is it useful here?
2. Without changing the fundamental design, critique the way this design was executed. What might you have done differently? What is the purpose of the `pimpl_` member?
3. This design can, in fact, be substantially improved. What are `GenericTableAlgorithm`'s responsibilities? If more than one, how could they be better encapsulated? Explain how your answer affects the class's reusability, especially its extensibility.

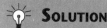

Solution

Let's consider the questions one by one.

1. This is a good design and implements a well-known design pattern. Which pattern is this? Why is it useful here?

This is the Template Method (Gamma95) pattern (not to be confused with C++ templates). It's useful because we can generalize a common way of doing something that always follows the same steps. Only the details may differ and can be supplied by a derived class. Further, a derived class may choose to reapply the same Template Method approach—that is, it may override the virtual function as a wrapper around a new virtual function—so different steps can be filled in at different levels in the class hierarchy.

(Note: The Pimpl Idiom is superficially similar to Bridge, but here it's only intended to hide this particular class's own implementation as a compilation dependency firewall, not to act as a true extensible bridge. We'll analyze the Pimpl Idiom in depth in Items 26 through 30.)

Guideline

Avoid public virtual functions; prefer using the Template Method pattern instead.

Guideline

Know about and use design patterns.

2. Without changing the fundamental design, critique the way this design was executed. What might you have done differently? What is the purpose of the `pimpl_` member?

This design uses `bool`s as return codes, with apparently no other way (status codes or exceptions) of reporting failures. Depending on the requirements, this may be fine, but it's something to note.

The (intentionally pronounceable) `pimpl_` member nicely hides the implementation behind an opaque pointer. The struct that `pimpl_` points to will contain the private member functions and member variables so that any change to them will not require client code to recompile. This is an important technique documented by Lakos (Lakos96) and others, because while it's a little annoying to code, it does help compensate for C++'s lack of a module system.

Guideline

For widely used classes, prefer to use the compiler-firewall idiom (Pimpl Idiom) to hide implementation details. Use an opaque pointer (a pointer to a declared but undefined class) declared as "`struct XxxxImpl; XxxxImpl* pimpl_;`" to store private members (including both state variables and member functions)—for example, "`class Map { private: struct MapImpl; MapImpl* pimpl_; };`".

3. This design can, in fact, be substantially improved. What are `GenericTableAlgorithm`'s responsibilities? If more than one, how could they be better encapsulated? Explain how your answer affects the class's reusability, especially its extensibility.

`GenericTableAlgorithm` can be substantially improved because it currently holds two jobs. Just as humans get stressed when they have to hold two jobs—because that means they're loaded up with extra and competing responsibilities—so too this class could benefit from adjusting its focus.

In the original version, `GenericTableAlgorithm` is burdened with two different and unrelated responsibilities that can be effectively separated, because the two responsibilities are to support entirely different audiences. In short, they are:

- Client code USES the (suitably specialized) generic algorithm.
- `GenericTableAlgorithm` USES the specialized concrete "details" class to specialize its operation for a specific case or usage.

Guideline

Prefer cohesion. Always endeavor to give each piece of code—each module, each class, each function—a single, well-defined responsibility.

That said, let's look at some improved code:

```
//---------------------------------------------------
// File gta.h
//---------------------------------------------------
// Responsibility #1: Providing a public interface
// that encapsulates common functionality as a
// template method. This has nothing to do with
// inheritance relationships, and can be nicely
// isolated to stand on its own in a better-focused
// class. The target audience is external users of
// GenericTableAlgorithm.
//
class GTAClient;

class GenericTableAlgorithm
{
public:
  // Constructor now takes a concrete implementation
  // object.
  //
  GenericTableAlgorithm( const string& table,
                         GTAClient&    worker );

  // Since we've separated away the inheritance
  // relationships, the destructor doesn't need to be
  // virtual.
  //
  ~GenericTableAlgorithm();

  bool Process(); // unchanged

private:
  struct GenericTableAlgorithmImpl* pimpl_; // MYOB
};

//---------------------------------------------------
// File gtaclient.h
//---------------------------------------------------
// Responsibility #2: Providing an abstract interface
// for extensibility. This is an implementation
// detail of GenericTableAlgorithm that has nothing
// to do with its external clients, and can be nicely
// separated out into a better-focused abstract
// protocol class. The target audience is writers of
// concrete "implementation detail" classes which
// work with (and extend) GenericTableAlgorithm.
//
class GTAClient
{
public:
  virtual ~GTAClient() =0;
  virtual bool Filter( const Record& );
  virtual bool ProcessRow( const PrimaryKey& ) =0;
};
```

```
//-------------------------------------------------
// File gtaclient.cpp
//-------------------------------------------------
bool GTAClient::Filter( const Record& )
{
  return true;
}
```

As shown, these two classes should appear in separate header files. With these changes, how does this now look to the client code? The answer is: pretty much the same.

```
class MyWorker : public GTAClient
{
  // ... override Filter() and ProcessRow() to
  //     implement a specific operation ...
};

int main()
{
  GenericTableAlgorithm a( "Customer", MyWorker() );
  a.Process();
}
```

While this may look pretty much the same, consider three important effects.

1. What if `GenericTableAlgorithm`'s common public interface changes (for example, a new public member is added)? In the original version, all concrete worker classes would have to be recompiled because they are derived from `GenericTableAlgorithm`. In this version, any change to `GenericTableAlgorithm`'s public interface is nicely isolated and does not affect the concrete worker classes at all.
2. What if `GenericTableAlgorithm`'s extensible protocol changes (for example, if additional defaulted arguments were added to `Filter()` or `ProcessRow()`)? In the original version, all external clients of `GenericTableAlgorithm` would have to be recompiled even though the public interface is unchanged, because a derivation interface is visible in the class definition. In this version, any changes to `GenericTableAlgorithm`'s extension protocol interface is nicely isolated and does not affect external users at all.
3. Any concrete worker classes can now be used within any other algorithm that can operate using the `Filter()/ProcessRow()` interface, not just `GenericTableAlgorithm`. In fact, what we've ended up with is very similar to the Strategy pattern.

Remember the computer science motto: Most problems can be solved by adding a level of indirection. Of course, it's wise to temper this with Occam's Razor: Don't make things more complex than necessary. A proper balance between the two in this case delivers much better reusability and maintainability at little or no cost—a good deal by all accounts.

Let's talk about more generic genericity for a moment. You may have noticed that `GenericTableAlgorithm` could actually be a function instead of a class (in fact, some people might be tempted to rename `Process()` as `operator()()`, because now the class apparently really is just a functor). The reason it could be replaced with a function is that the description doesn't say that it needs to keep state across calls to `Process()`. For example, if it does not need to keep state across invocations, we could replace it with:

```
bool GenericTableAlgorithm(
  const string& table,
  GTAClient&    method
  )
{
  // ... original contents of Process() go here ...
}

int main()
{
  GenericTableAlgorithm( "Customer", MyWorker() );
}
```

What we've really got here is a generic function, which can be given "specialized" behaviour as needed. If you know that `method` objects never need to store state (that is, all instances are functionally equivalent and provide only the virtual functions), you can get fancy and make `method` a nonclass template parameter instead.

```
template<typename GTACworker>
bool GenericTableAlgorithm( const string& table )
{
  // ... original contents of Process() go here ...
}

int main()
{
  GenericTableAlgorithm<MyWorker>( "Customer" );
}
```

I don't think that this buys you much here besides getting rid of a comma in the client code, so the first function is better. It's always good to resist the temptation to write cute code for its own sake.

At any rate, whether to use a function or a class in a given situation can depend on what you're trying to achieve, but in this case writing a generic function may be a better solution.

Item 24: Uses and Abuses of Inheritance — Difficulty: 6

"Why inherit?"

Inheritance is often overused, even by experienced developers. Always minimize coupling. If a class relationship can be expressed in more than one way, use the weakest relationship that's practical. Given that inheritance is nearly the strongest relationship you can express in C++ (second only to friendship), it's only really appropriate when there is no equivalent weaker alternative.

In this Item, the spotlight is on private inheritance, one real (if obscure) use for protected inheritance, and a recap of the proper use of public inheritance. Along the way, we will create a fairly complete list of all the usual and unusual reasons to use inheritance.

The following template provides list-management functions, including the ability to manipulate list elements at specific list locations.

```
// Example 1
//
template <class T>
class MyList
{
public:
  bool   Insert( const T&, size_t index );
  T      Access( size_t index ) const;
  size_t Size() const;
private:
  T*     buf_;
  size_t bufsize_;
};
```

Consider the following code, which shows two ways to write a `MySet` class in terms of `MyList`. Assume that all important elements are shown.

```
// Example 1(a)
//
template <class T>
class MySet1 : private MyList<T>
{
public:
  bool   Add( const T& ); // calls Insert()
  T      Get( size_t index ) const;
                          // calls Access()
  using MyList<T>::Size;
  //...
};

// Example 1(b)
//
template <class T>
class MySet2
{
public:
  bool   Add( const T& ); // calls impl_.Insert()
  T      Get( size_t index ) const;
                          // calls impl_.Access()
  size_t Size() const;    // calls impl_.Size();
  //...
private:
  MyList<T> impl_;
};
```

Give these alternatives some thought, and consider the following questions.

1. Is there any difference between `MySet1` and `MySet2`?
2. More generally, what *is* the difference between nonpublic inheritance and containment? Make as comprehensive a list as you can of reasons why you would use inheritance instead of containment.

3. Which version of `MySet` would you prefer—`MySet1` or `MySet2`?
4. Finally, make as comprehensive a list as you can of reasons why you would use public inheritance.

Solution

This motivating example helps to illustrate some of the issues surrounding the use of inheritance, especially how to choose between nonpublic inheritance and containment.

The answer to Question 1—Is there any difference between `MySet1` and `MySet2`—is straightforward: There is no substantial difference between `MySet1` and `MySet2`. They are functionally identical.

Question 2 gets us right down to business: More generally, what *is* the difference between nonpublic inheritance and containment? Make as comprehensive a list as you can of reasons why you would use inheritance instead of containment.

- *Nonpublic inheritance* should always express IS-IMPLEMENTED-IN-TERMS-OF (with only one rare exception, which I'll cover shortly). It makes the using class depend upon the public *and protected* parts of the used class.
- *Containment* always expresses HAS-A and, therefore, IS-IMPLEMENTED-IN-TERMS-OF. It makes the using class depend upon only the public parts of the used class.

It's easy to show that inheritance is a superset of single containment—that is, there's nothing we can do with a single `MyList<T>` member that we couldn't do if we inherited from `MyList<T>`. Of course, using inheritance does limit us to having just one `MyList<T>` (as a base subobject); if we needed to have multiple instances of `MyList<T>`, we would have to use containment instead.

Guideline

Prefer containment (a.k.a. "composition", "layering", "HAS-A", "delegation") to inheritance. When modeling IS-IMPLEMENTED-IN-TERMS-OF, always prefer expressing it using containment, not inheritance.

That being the case, what are the extra things we can do if we use inheritance that we can't do if we use containment? In other words, why use nonpublic inheritance? Here are several reasons, in rough order from most to least common. Interestingly, the final item points out a useful(?) application of protected inheritance.

- *We need to override a virtual function.* This is one of inheritance's classic *raisons d'être.*[7] Often, we want to override in order to customize the used class's behavior. Sometimes, however, there's no other choice. If the used class is abstract—that is, it has at least one pure virtual function that has not yet been overridden—we must inherit and override because we can't instantiate directly.

7. See also Meyers98 under the index entry, "French, gratuitous use of."

- *We need access to a protected member.* This applies to protected member functions[8] in general, and to protected constructors in particular.
- *We need to construct the used object before, or destroy it after, another base subobject.* If the slightly longer object lifetime matters, there's no way to get it other than by using inheritance. This can be necessary when the used class provides a lock of some sort, such as a critical section or a database transaction, which must cover the entire lifetime of another base subobject.
- *We need to share a common virtual base class or override the construction of a virtual base class.* The first part applies if the using class has to inherit from one of the same virtual bases as the used class. If it does not, the second part may still apply. The most-derived class is responsible for initializing all virtual base classes, so if we need to use a different constructor or different constructor parameters for a virtual base, then we must inherit.
- *We benefit substantially from the empty base class optimization.* Sometimes, the class you are IMPLEMENTING-IN-TERMS-OF may have no data members at all—that is, it's just a bundle of functions. In this case, there can be a space advantage to using inheritance instead of containment because of the empty base class optimization. In short, compilers are allowed to let an empty base subobject occupy zero space; whereas an empty member object must occupy nonzero space, even if it doesn't have any data.

```
class B { /* ... functions only, no data ... */ };
// Containment: incurs some space overhead
//
class D
{
  B b_; // b_ must occupy at least one byte,
};      // even though B is an empty class
// Inheritance: can incur zero space overhead
//
class D : private B
{       // the B base subobject need not
};      // occupy any space at all
```

For a detailed discussion of the empty base optimization, see Nathan Myers' excellent article on this topic in *Dr. Dobb's Journal* (Myers97).

Having said all that, let me add a caution for the overzealous: Not all compilers actually perform the empty base class optimization. And even if they do, you probably won't benefit significantly unless you know there will be many (say, tens of thousands) of these objects in your system. Unless the space savings are very important to your application and you know that your compiler will actually perform the optimization, it would be a mistake to introduce the extra coupling of the stronger inheritance relationship instead of using simple containment.

8. I say "member functions" because you would never write a class that has a public or protected member variable, right? (Regardless of the poor example set by some libraries.)

There is one additional feature we can get using nonpublic inheritance, and it's the only one that doesn't model IS-IMPLEMENTED-IN-TERMS-OF:

- *We need "controlled polymorphism"—LSP IS-A, but in certain code only.* Public inheritance should always model IS-A as per the Liskov Substitution Principle (LSP).[9] Nonpublic inheritance can express a restricted form of IS-A, even though most people identify IS-A with public inheritance alone. Given `class Derived : private Base`, from the point of view of outside code, a `Derived` object IS-NOT-A `Base`. So, of course, it can't be used polymorphically as a `Base` because of the access restrictions imposed by private inheritance. However, *inside* `Derived`'s own member functions and friends only, a `Derived` object can indeed be used polymorphically as a `Base` (you can supply a pointer or reference to a `Derived` object where a `Base` object is expected), because members and friends have the necessary access. If instead of private inheritance, you use protected inheritance, then the IS-A relationship is more visible to further-derived classes, which means subclasses can also make use of the polymorphism.

That's as complete a list as I can make of reasons to use nonpublic inheritance. (In fact, just one additional point would make this a complete list of all reasons to use any kind of inheritance: We need public inheritance to express IS-A. More on that when we get to Question 4.)

All of this brings us to Question 3: Which version of `MySet` would you prefer—`MySet1` or `MySet2`? Let's analyze the code in Example 1 and see whether any of the above criteria apply.

- `MyList` has no protected members, so we don't need to inherit to gain access to them.
- `MyList` has no virtual functions, so we don't need to inherit to override them.
- `MySet` has no other potential base classes, so the `MyList` object doesn't need to be constructed before, or destroyed after, another base subobject.
- `MyList` has no virtual base classes that `MySet` might need to share or whose construction it might need to override.
- `MyList` is nonempty, so the "empty base class optimization" motive does not apply.
- `MySet` IS-NOT-A `MyList`, not even within `MySet`'s member functions and friends. This last point is interesting, because it points out a (minor) disadvantage of inheritance. Even had one of the other criteria been true so that we would use inheritance, we would have to be careful that members and friends of `MySet` wouldn't accidentally use a `MySet` polymorphically as a `MyList`—a remote possibility, maybe, but sufficiently subtle that if it did ever happen, it would probably keep the poor programmer who encountered it confused for hours.

In short, `MySet` should not inherit from `MyList`. Using inheritance where containment is just as effective only introduces gratuitous coupling and needless dependencies, and that's never a good idea. Unfortunately, in the real world, I still see programmers—even experienced ones—who implement relationships like `MySet`'s using inheritance.

---

9. See `www.gotw.ca/publications/xc++/om.htm` for several good papers describing LSP.

Astute readers will have noticed that the inheritance-based version of `MySet` does offer one (fairly trivial) advantage over the containment-based version: Using inheritance, you need to write only a `using`-declaration to expose the unchanged `Size` function. Using containment, you have to explicitly write a simple forwarding function to get the same effect.

Of course, sometimes inheritance will be appropriate. For example:

```
// Example 2: Sometimes you need to inherit
//
class Base
{
public:
  virtual int Func1();
protected:
  bool Func2();
private:
  bool Func3(); // uses Func1
};
```

If we need to override a virtual function like `Func1` or access a protected member like `Func2`, inheritance is necessary. Example 2 illustrates why overriding a virtual function may be necessary for reasons other than allowing polymorphism. Here, `Base` is implemented in terms of `Func1` (`Func3` uses `Func1` in its implementation), so the only way to get the right behavior is to override `Func1`. Even when inheritance is necessary, however, is the following the right way to do it?

```
// Example 2(a)
//
class Derived : private Base // necessary?
{
public:
  int Func1();
  // ... more functions, some of which use
  //     Base::Func2(), some of which don't ...
};
```

This code allows `Derived` to override `Base::Func1`, which is good. Unfortunately, it also grants access to `Base::Func2` *to all members of* `Derived`, and there's the rub. Maybe only a few, or just one, of `Derived`'s member functions really need access to `Base::Func2`. By using inheritance like this, we've needlessly made all of `Derived`'s members depend upon `Base`'s protected interface.

Clearly, inheritance is necessary, but wouldn't it be nice to introduce only as much coupling as we really need? Well, we can do better with a little judicious engineering.

```
// Example 2(b)
//
class DerivedImpl : private Base
{
public:
  int Func1();
  // ... functions that use Func2 ...
```

```
};
class Derived
{
  // ... functions that don't use Func2 ...
private:
  DerivedImpl impl_;
};
```

This design is much better, because it nicely separates and encapsulates the dependencies on `Base`. `Derived` only depends directly on `Base`'s public interface and on `DerivedImpl`'s public interface. Why is this design more successful? Primarily, because it follows the fundamental "one class, one responsibility" design guideline. In Example 2(a), `Derived` was responsible for both customizing `Base` and implementing itself in terms of `Base`. In Example 2(b), those concerns are nicely separated out.

Now for some variants on containment. Containment has some advantages of its own. First, it allows having multiple instances of the used class, which isn't practical, or even always possible, with inheritance. If you need to both derive and have multiple instances, just use the same idiom as in Example 2(b). Derive a helper class (like `DerivedImpl`) to do whatever needs the inheritance, then contain multiple copies of the helper class.

Second, having the used class be a data member gives additional flexibility. The member can be hidden behind a compiler firewall inside a Pimpl[10] (whereas base class definitions must always be visible), and it can be easily converted to a pointer if it needs to be changed at run-time (whereas inheritance hierarchies are static and fixed at compile-time).

Finally, here's a third useful way to rewrite `MySet2` from Example 1(b) to use containment in a more generic way.

```
// Example 1(c): Generic containment
//
template <class T, class Impl = MyList<T> >
class MySet3
{
public:
  bool   Add( const T& ); // calls impl_.Insert()
  T      Get( size_t index ) const;
                          // calls impl_.Access()
  size_t Size() const;    // calls impl_.Size();
  // ...
private:
  Impl impl_;
};
```

Instead of just choosing to be IMPLEMENTED-IN-TERMS-OF `MyList<T>` only, we now have the flexibility of having `MySet` IMPLEMENT*ABLE*-IN-TERMS-OF any class that supports the required `Add`, `Get`, and other functions that we need. The C++ standard library uses this very technique for its `stack` and `queue` templates, which are by default IMPLEMENTED-IN-TERMS-OF a `deque`, but are also IMPLEMENT*ABLE*-IN-TERMS-OF any other class that provides the required services.

10. See Items 26 through 30.

Specifically, different user code may choose to instantiate `MySet` using implementations with different performance characteristics—for example, if I know I'm going to write code that does many more inserts than searches, I'd want to use an implementation that optimizes inserts. We haven't lost any ease of use, either. Under Example 1(b), client code could simply write `MySet2<int>` to instantiate a set of `int`s, and that's still true with Example 1(c), because `MySet3<int>` is just a synonym for `MySet3<int,MyList<int> >`, thanks to the default template parameter.

This kind of flexibility is more difficult to achieve with inheritance, primarily because inheritance tends to fix an implementation decision at design time. It is possible to write Example 1(c) to inherit from `Impl`, but here the tighter coupling isn't necessary and should be avoided.

The most important thing to know about public inheritance can be learned with the answer to Question 4: Make as comprehensive a list as you can of reasons why you would use public inheritance.

There is only one point I want to stress about public inheritance, and if you follow this advice it will steer you clear of the most common abuses. *Only* use public inheritance to model true IS-A, as per the Liskov Substitution Principle.[11] That is, a publicly derived class object should be able to be used in any context in which the base class object could be used and still guarantee the same semantics. [Note: We covered a rare exception—or, more correctly, an *extension*—to this idea in Item 3.]

In particular, following this rule will avoid two common pitfalls.

- *Never use public inheritance when nonpublic inheritance will do.* Public inheritance should never be used to model IS-IMPLEMENTED-IN-TERMS-OF without true IS-A. This may seem obvious, but I've noticed that some programmers routinely make inheritance public out of habit. That's not a good idea, and this point is in the same spirit as my advice to never use inheritance (of any kind) when good old containment/membership will do. If the extra access and tighter coupling aren't needed, why use them? If a class relationship can be expressed in more than one way, use the weakest relationship that's practical.
- *Never use public inheritance to implement "IS-ALMOST-A."* I've seen some programmers, even experienced ones, inherit publicly from a base and implement "most" of the overridden virtual functions in a way that preserved the semantics of the base class. In other words, in some cases using the `Derived` object as a `Base` would not behave quite the way that a reasonable `Base` client could expect. An example often cited by Robert Martin is the usually misguided idea of inheriting a `Square` class from a `Rectangle` class "because a square is a rectangle." That may be true in mathematics, but it's not necessarily true in classes. For example, say that the `Rectangle` class has a `virtual SetWidth(int)` function. Then `Square`'s implementation to set the width would also naturally set the height so that the object remains square. Yet there may well exist code elsewhere in the system that works polymorphically with `Rectangle` objects, and would not expect that changing the width would also change the height. After all, that's not true of `Rectangle`s in general! This is a good example of public inheritance that would

11. See `www.gotw.ca/publications/xc++/om.htm` for several good papers describing LSP.

violate LSP, because the derived class does not deliver the same semantics as the base class. It violates the key precept of public inheritance: "Require no more and promise no less."

When I see people doing this kind of "almost IS-A," I usually try to point out to them that they're setting themselves up for trouble. After all, someone, somewhere is bound to try to use derived objects polymorphically in one of the ways that would occasionally give unexpected results, right? "But it's okay," came one reply, "it's only a little bit incompatible, and I know that nobody uses `Base`-family objects in that way [that would be dangerous]." Well, being "a little bit incompatible" is a lot like being "a little bit pregnant." Now, I had no reason to doubt that the programmer was right—namely, that no code then in the system would hit the dangerous differences. However, I also had every reason to believe that someday, somewhere, a maintenance programmer was going to make a seemingly innocuous change, run afoul of the problem, and spend hours analyzing why the class was poorly designed and then spend additional days fixing it.

Don't be tempted. Just say no. If it doesn't behave like a `Base`, it's NOT-A `Base`, so don't derive and make it look like one.

> **Guideline**
>
> *Always ensure that public inheritance models both IS-A and WORKS-LIKE-A according to the Liskov Substitution Principle. All overridden member functions must require no more and promise no less.*

> **Guideline**
>
> *Never inherit publicly to reuse (code in the base class); inherit publicly in order to be reused (by existing code that uses base objects polymorphically).*

Conclusion

Use inheritance wisely. If you can express a class relationship using containment/delegation alone, you should always prefer that. If you need inheritance but aren't modeling IS-A, use nonpublic inheritance. If you don't need the combinative power of multiple inheritance, prefer single inheritance. Large inheritance hierarchies, in general, and deep ones, in particular, are confusing to understand and therefore difficult to maintain. Inheritance is a design-time decision and trades off a lot of run-time flexibility.

Some people feel that "it just isn't OO unless you inherit," but that isn't really true. Use the simplest solution that works, and you'll be more likely to enjoy many pleasant years of stable and maintainable code.

Item 25: Object-Oriented Programming Difficulty: 4

Is C++ an object-oriented language? It both is and is not, contrary to popular opinion. For a change of pace (and to get a brief break from staring at code), here is an essay question. Don't just turn quickly to the answer—give it some thought.

"C++ is a powerful language that provides many advanced object-oriented constructs, including encapsulation, exception handling, inheritance, templates, polymorphism, strong typing, and a complete module system."

Discuss.

Solution

The purpose of this Item was to provoke thought about major (and even missing) features in C++, and to provide a healthy dose of reality. Specifically, I hope that your thinking about this Item has generated ideas and examples that illustrate three main things.

1. *Not everyone agrees about what OO means.* "Well, what *is* object orientation, anyway?" Even at this late date, if you ask 10 people, you're likely to get 15 different answers. (Not much better than asking 10 lawyers for legal opinions.)

Just about everyone would agree that inheritance and polymorphism are OO concepts. Most people would include encapsulation. A few might include exception handling, and perhaps no one would include templates. The point is that there are differing opinions on whether any given feature is OO, and each viewpoint has its passionate defenders.

2. *C++ is a multiparadigm language.* C++ is not just an OO language. It supports many OO features, but it doesn't force programmers to use them. You can write completely non-OO programs in C++, and many people do.

The C++ standardization effort's most important contribution to C++ is stronger support for *powerful abstraction* to reduce software complexity (Martin95).[12] C++ is not solely an object-oriented language. It supports several programming styles, including both object-oriented programming and generic programming. These styles are fundamentally important because each provides flexible ways to organize code through abstraction. Object-oriented programming lets us bundle an object's state together with the functions that manipulate it, and encapsulation and inheritance let us manage interdependencies and make reuse cleaner and easier. Generic programming is a more recent style that lets us

12. The book contains an excellent discussion of why one of object-oriented programming's most important benefits is that it lets us reduce software complexity by managing code interdependencies.

write functions and classes that operate on other functions and objects of unspecified, unrelated, and unknown types, providing a unique way to reduce coupling and interdependencies within a program. A few other languages currently provide support for genericity, but none yet support it as strongly as C++. Indeed, modern generic programming was made possible by the unique C++ formulation of templates.

Today, C++ provides many powerful ways to express abstraction, and the resulting flexibility is the most important result of C++ standardization.

3. *No language is the be-all and end-all.* Today, I'm using C++ as my primary programming language; tomorrow, I'll use whatever best suits what I'm doing then. C++ does not have a module system (complete or otherwise); it lacks other major features, such as garbage collection; and it has static typing, but not necessarily "strong" typing. All languages have advantages and drawbacks. Just pick the right tool for the job, and avoid the temptation to become a nearsighted language zealot.

Compiler Firewalls and the Pimpl Idiom

Managing dependencies well is an essential part of writing solid code. I've argued (Sutter98) that C++'s greatest strength is that it supports two powerful methods of abstraction: object-oriented programming and generic programming. Both are fundamentally tools to help manage dependencies and, therefore, manage complexity. It's telling that all of the common OO/generic buzzwords—including encapsulation, polymorphism, and type independence—and all the design patterns I know of describe ways to manage complexity within a software system by managing the code's interdependencies.

Item 26: Minimizing Compile-time Dependencies—Part 1 — Difficulty: 4

When we talk about dependencies, we usually think of run-time dependencies like class interactions. In this Item, we will focus instead on how to analyze and manage compile-time dependencies. As a first step, try to identify (and root out) unnecessary headers.

Many programmers habitually `#include` many more headers than necessary. Unfortunately, doing so can seriously degrade build times, especially when a popular header file includes too many other headers.

In the following header file, which `#include` directives could be immediately removed without ill effect? You may not make any changes other than removing or rewriting `#include` directives. Note that the comments are important.

```
//  x.h: original header
//
#include <iostream>
#include <ostream>
#include <list>
```

```
// None of A, B, C, D or E are templates.
// Only A and C have virtual functions.
#include "a.h"  // class A
#include "b.h"  // class B
#include "c.h"  // class C
#include "d.h"  // class D
#include "e.h"  // class E
class X : public A, private B
{
public:
     X( const C& );
  B  f( int, char* );
  C  f( int, C );
  C& g( B );
  E  h( E );
  virtual std::ostream& print( std::ostream& ) const;
private:
  std::list<C> clist_;
  D            d_;
};
inline std::ostream& operator<<( std::ostream& os, const X& x )
{
  return x.print(os);
}
```

Solution

Of the first two standard headers mentioned in `x.h`, one can be immediately removed because it's not needed at all, and the second can be replaced with a smaller header.

1. Remove `iostream`.

```
#include <iostream>
```

Many programmers `#include <iostream>` purely out of habit as soon as they see anything resembling a stream nearby. `X` does make use of streams, that's true; but it doesn't mention anything specifically from `iostream`. At the most, `X` needs `ostream` alone, and even that can be whittled down.

Guideline

Never `#include` unnecessary header files.

2. Replace `ostream` with `iosfwd`.

```
#include < ostream >
```

Parameter and return types need only to be forward-declared, so instead of the full definition of `ostream` we really only need its forward declaration.

In the old days, you could just replace "`#include <ostream>`" with "`class ostream;`" in this situation, because `ostream` used to be a class and it wasn't in `namespace std`. Alas, no more. Writing "`class ostream;`" is illegal for two reasons.

1. `ostream` is now in `namespace std`, and programmers aren't allowed to declare anything that lives in `namespace std`.
2. `ostream` is now a `typedef` of a template; specifically, it's `typedef`'d as `basic_ostream<char>`. Not only would the `basic_ostream` template be messy to forward-declare in any case, but you couldn't reliably forward-declare it at all, because library implementations are allowed to do things like add their own extra template parameters (beyond those required by the standard), which, of course, your code wouldn't know about—one of the primary reasons for the rule that programmers aren't allowed to write their own declarations for things in `namespace std`.

All is not lost, however. The standard library helpfully provides the header `iosfwd`, which contains forward declarations for all the stream templates (including `basic_ostream`) and their standard `typedef`s (including `ostream`). So all we need to do is replace "`#include <ostream>`" with "`#include <iosfwd>`".

Guideline

Prefer to `#include <iosfwd>` when a forward declaration of a stream will suffice.

Incidentally, once you see `iosfwd`, one might think that the same trick would work for other standard library templates, such as `list` and `string`. There are, however, no comparable "`stringfwd`" or "`listfwd`" standard headers. The `iosfwd` header was created to give streams special treatment for backward compatibility, to avoid breaking code written in years past for the "old" nontemplated version of the iostreams subsystem.

There, that was easy. We can…

What? "Not so fast!" I hear some of you say. "This header does a lot more with `ostream` than just mention it as a parameter or return type. The inlined `operator<<` actually uses an `ostream` object! So it must need `ostream`'s definition, right?"

That's a reasonable question. Happily, the answer is: No, it doesn't. Consider again the function in question:

```
inline std::ostream& operator<<( std::ostream& os, const X& x )
{
  return x.print(os);
}
```

This function mentions an `ostream&` as both a parameter and a return type (which most people know doesn't require a definition), and it passes its `ostream&` parameter in turn as a parameter to another function (which many people *don't* know doesn't require a definition either). As long as that's all we're doing with the `ostream&`, there's no need for a full `ostream` definition. Of course, we would need the full definition if we tried to call any member functions, for example, but we're not doing anything like that here.

So, as I was saying, we can get rid of only one of the other headers just yet.

3. Replace `e.h` with a forward declaration.

```
#include "e.h"  // class E
```

Class `E` is just being mentioned as a parameter and as a return type, so no definition is required, and `x.h` shouldn't be pulling in `e.h` in the first place. All we need to do is replace "`#include "e.h"`" with "`class E;`".

Guideline

Never `#include` a header when a forward declaration will suffice.

Item 27: Minimizing Compile-time Dependencies—Part 2 — Difficulty: 6

Now that the unnecessary headers have been removed, it's time for Phase 2: How can you limit dependencies on the internals of a class?

Below is how the header from Item 26 looks after the initial clean-up pass. What further `#include`s could be removed if we made some suitable changes, and how?

This time, you may make changes to `X` as long as `X`'s base classes and its public interface remain unchanged; any current code that already uses `X` should not be affected beyond requiring a simple recompilation.

```
//  x.h: sans gratuitous headers
//
#include <iosfwd>
#include <list>
// None of A, B, C or D are templates.
// Only A and C have virtual functions.
#include "a.h"  // class A
#include "b.h"  // class B
#include "c.h"  // class C
#include "d.h"  // class D
class E;
class X : public A, private B
{
public:
     X( const C& );
  B  f( int, char* );
  C  f( int, C );
```

```
    C& g( B );
    E  h( E );
    virtual std::ostream& print( std::ostream& ) const;
  private:
    std::list<C> clist_;
    D            d_;
  };
  inline std::ostream& operator<<( std::ostream& os, const X& x )
  {
    return x.print(os);
  }
```

Solution

There are a couple of things we weren't able to do in the previous problem.

- We had to leave `a.h` and `b.h`. We couldn't get rid of these because `X` inherits from both `A` and `B`, and you always have to have full definitions for base classes so that the compiler can determine `X`'s object size, virtual functions, and other fundamentals. (Can you anticipate how to remove one of these? Think about it: Which one can you remove, and why/how? The answer will come shortly.)
- We had to leave `list`, `c.h`, and `d.h`. We couldn't get rid of these right away because a `list<C>` and a `D` appear as private data members of `X`. Although `C` appears as neither a base class nor a member, it is being used to instantiate the `list` member, and most current compilers require that when you instantiate `list<C>`, you are able to see the definition of `C`. (The standard doesn't require a definition here, though, so even if the compiler you are currently using has this restriction, you can expect the restriction to go away over time.)

Now let's talk about the beauty of Pimpls. (Yes, really.)

C++ lets us easily encapsulate the private parts of a class from unauthorized *access*. Unfortunately, because of the header file approach inherited from C, it can take a little more work to encapsulate *dependencies* on a class's privates. "But," you say, "the whole point of encapsulation is that the client code shouldn't have to know or care about a class's private implementation details, right?" Right, and in C++, the client code doesn't need to know or care about access to a class's privates (because unless it's a friend, it isn't allowed any), but because the privates are visible in the header, the client code does have to depend upon any types they mention.

How can we better insulate clients from a class's private implementation details? One good way is to use a special form of the handle/body idiom (Coplien92) (what I call the Pimpl Idiom because of the intentionally pronounceable `pimpl_` pointer[1]) as a compilation firewall (Lakos96, Meyers98, Meyers99, Murray93).

1. I always used to write `impl_`. The eponymous `pimpl_` was actually coined several years ago by Jeff Sumner (chief programmer at PeerDirect), due in equal parts to a penchant for Hungarian-style "p" prefixes for pointer variables and an occasional taste for horrid puns.

A Pimpl is just an opaque pointer (a pointer to a forward-declared, but undefined, helper class) used to hide the private members of a class. That is, instead of writing:

```
// file x.h
class X
{
  // public and protected members
private:
  // private members; whenever these change,
  // all client code must be recompiled
};
```

we write:

```
// file x.h
class X
{
  // public and protected members
private:
  struct XImpl;
  XImpl* pimpl_;
    // a pointer to a forward-declared class
};

// file x.cpp
struct X::XImpl
{
  // private members; fully hidden, can be
  // changed at will without recompiling clients
};
```

Every `X` object dynamically allocates its `XImpl` object. If you think of an object as a physical block, we've essentially lopped off a large chunk of the block and in its place left only "a little bump on the side"—the opaque pointer, or Pimpl.

The major advantages of this idiom come from the fact that it breaks compile-time dependencies.

- Types mentioned only in a class's implementation need no longer be defined for client code, which can eliminate extra `#include`s and improve compile speeds.
- A class's implementation can be changed—that is, private members can be freely added or removed, without recompiling client code.

The major costs of this idiom are in performance.

- Each construction/destruction must allocate/deallocate memory.
- Each access of a hidden member can require at least one extra indirection. (If the hidden member being accessed itself uses a back pointer to call a function in the visible class, there will be multiple indirections.)

We'll come back to these and other Pimpl issues later in this section. For now, in our example, there were three headers whose definitions were needed simply because they appeared as private members of X. If we instead restructure X to use a Pimpl, we can immediately make several further simplifications.

Use the Pimpl idiom to hide the private implementation details of X.

```
#include <list>

#include "c.h"  // class C
#include "d.h"  // class D
```

One of these headers (c.h) can be replaced with a forward declaration, because C is still being mentioned elsewhere as a parameter or return type, and the other two (list and d.h) can disappear completely.

Guideline

For widely used classes, prefer to use the compiler-firewall idiom (Pimpl Idiom) to hide implementation details. Use an opaque pointer (a pointer to a declared, but undefined, class) declared as "`struct XxxxImpl; XxxxImpl* pimpl_;`" to store private members (including both state variables and member functions). For example: "`class Map { private: struct MapImpl; MapImpl* pimpl_; };`".

After making that additional change, the header looks like this:

```
//  x.h: after converting to use a Pimpl
//
#include <iosfwd>
#include "a.h"  // class A (has virtual functions)
#include "b.h"  // class B (has no virtual functions)
class C;
class E;
class X : public A, private B
{
public:
     X( const C& );
  B  f( int, char* );
  C  f( int, C );
  C& g( B );
  E  h( E );
  virtual std::ostream& print( std::ostream& ) const;
private:
  struct XImpl;
  XImpl* pimpl_;
    // opaque pointer to forward-declared class
};
inline std::ostream& operator<<( std::ostream& os, const X& x )
{
  return x.print(os);
}
```

The private details go into X's implementation file, where client code never sees them and therefore never depends upon them.

```
//  Implementation file x.cpp
//
struct X::XImpl
{
  std::list<C> clist_;
  D            d_;
};
```

That brings us down to including only three headers, which is a great improvement. But it turns out that there is still a little more we could do, if only we were allowed to change the structure of X more extensively. This leads us nicely into Item 28…

Item 28: Minimizing Compile-time Dependencies—Part 3 — Difficulty: 7

Now the unnecessary headers have been removed, and needless dependencies on the internals of the class have been eliminated. Is there any further decoupling that can be done? The answer takes us back to basic principles of solid class design.

The Incredible Shrinking Header has now been greatly trimmed, but there may still be ways to reduce the dependencies further. What further `#include`s could be removed if we made further changes to X, and how?

This time, you may make any changes to X as long as they don't change its public interface so that existing code that uses X is unaffected beyond requiring a simple recompilation. Again, note that the comments are important.

```
//  x.h: after converting to use a Pimpl
//       to hide implementation details
//

#include <iosfwd>
#include "a.h"  // class A (has virtual functions)
#include "b.h"  // class B (has no virtual functions)
class C;
class E;

class X : public A, private B
{
public:
     X( const C& );
  B  f( int, char* );
  C  f( int, C );
```

```
    C& g( B );
    E  h( E );
    virtual std::ostream& print( std::ostream& ) const;
  private:
    struct XImpl;
    XImpl* pimpl_;
      // opaque pointer to forward-declared class
  };

  inline std::ostream& operator<<( std::ostream& os, const X& x )
  {
    return x.print(os);
  }
```

Solution

In my experience, many C++ programmers still seem to march to the "it isn't OO unless you inherit" battle hymn, by which I mean that they use inheritance more than necessary. See Item 24 for the whole exhausting lecture; the bottom line is simply that inheritance (including, but not limited to, IS-A) is a much stronger relationship than HAS-A or USES-A. When it comes to managing dependencies, therefore, you should always prefer composition/membership over inheritance. To paraphrase Albert Einstein: "Use as strong a relationship as necessary, but no stronger."

In this code, X is derived publicly from A and privately from B. Recall that public inheritance should always model IS-A and satisfy the Liskov Substitution Principle.[2] In this case, X IS-A A and there's naught wrong with it, so we'll leave that as it is.

But did you notice the interesting thing about B?

The interesting thing about B is this: B is a private base class of X, but B has no virtual functions. Now, usually, the only reason you would choose private inheritance over composition/membership is to gain access to protected members—which most times means "to override a virtual function."[3] As we see, B has no virtual functions, so there's probably no reason to prefer the stronger relationship of inheritance (unless X needs access to some protected function or data in B, of course, but for now I'll assume this is not the case). Assuming that is, indeed, the case, however, instead of having a base subobject of type B, X probably ought to have simply a member object of type B. Therefore, the way to further simplify the header is remove unnecessary inheritance from class B.

```
#include "b.h"  // class B (has no virtual functions)
```

2. For lots of good discussion about applying the LSP, see the papers available online at www.gotw.ca/publications/xc++/om.htm, as well as Martin95.
3. Yes, there are other possible reasons to inherit, but the situations where those arise are rare and/or obscure. See Sutter98(a) and Sutter99 for an extensive discussion of the (few) reasons to use inheritance of any kind. Those articles point out in detail why containment/membership should often be used instead of inheritance.

Because the B member object should be private (it is, after all, an implementation detail), this member should live in X's hidden pimpl_ portion.

Guideline

Never inherit when composition is sufficient.

This leaves us with vastly simplified header code.

```
//  x.h: after removing unnecessary inheritance
//
#include <iosfwd>
#include "a.h"  // class A
class B;
class C;
class E;
class X : public A
{
public:
     X( const C& );
  B  f( int, char* );
  C  f( int, C );
  C& g( B );
  E  h( E );
  virtual std::ostream& print( std::ostream& ) const;
private:
  struct XImpl;
  XImpl* pimpl_; // this now quietly includes a B
};
inline std::ostream& operator<<( std::ostream& os, const X& x )
{
  return x.print(os);
}
```

After three passes of progressively greater simplification, the final result is that x.h is still using other class names all over the place, but clients of X need only pay for two #includes: a.h and iosfwd. What an improvement over the original!

Item 29: Compilation Firewalls — Difficulty: 6

Using the Pimpl Idiom can dramatically reduce code interdependencies and build times. But what should go into a `pimpl_` object, and what is the safest way to use it?

In C++, when anything in a class definition changes (even private members), all users of that class must be recompiled. To reduce these dependencies, a common technique is to use an opaque pointer to hide some of the implementation details.

```
class X
{
public:
  /* ... public members ... */
protected:
  /* ... protected members? ... */
private:
  /* ... private members? ... */
  struct XImpl;
  XImpl* pimpl_;          // opaque pointer to
                          // forward-declared class
};
```

The questions for you to answer are:

1. What should go into `XImpl`? There are four common disciplines.
   - Put all private data (but not functions) into `XImpl`.
   - Put all private members into `XImpl`.
   - Put all private and protected members into `XImpl`.
   - Make `XImpl` entirely the class that `X` would have been, and write `X` as only the public interface made up entirely of simple forwarding functions (a handle/body variant).

   What are the advantages/drawbacks of each? How would you choose among them?

2. Does `XImpl` require a pointer back to the `X` object?

Solution

Class `X` uses a variant of the handle/body idiom. As documented by Coplien (Coplien92), handle/body was described as primarily useful for reference counting of a shared implementation, but it also has more-general implementation-hiding uses. For convenience, from now on I'll call `X` the "visible class" and `XImpl` the "Pimpl class."

One big advantage of this idiom is that it breaks compile-time dependencies. First, system builds run faster, because using a Pimpl can eliminate extra `#includes` as demonstrated in Items 27 and 28. I have worked on projects in which converting just a few widely-visible classes to use Pimpls halved the system's build time. Second, it localizes the build impact of code changes because the parts of a class that reside in the Pimpl can be freely changed—that is, members can be freely added or removed—without recompiling client code.

Let's answer the Item questions one at a time.

1. What should go into `XImpl`?

Option 1 (Score: 6 / 10): Put all private data (but not functions) into `XImpl`. This is a good start, because it hides any class that appeared only as a data member. Still, we can usually do better.

Option 2 (Score: 10 / 10): Put all nonvirtual private members into `XImpl`. This is (almost) my usual practice these days. After all, in C++, the phrase "client code shouldn't and doesn't care about these parts" is spelled "`private`"—and privates are always hidden.[4]

There are some caveats.

- You can't hide virtual member functions in the Pimpl, even if the virtual functions are private. If the virtual function overrides one inherited from a base class, then it must appear in the actual derived class. If the virtual function is not inherited, then it must still appear in the visible class in order to be available for overriding by further derived classes.

  Virtual functions should normally be private, except that they have to be protected if a derived class's version needs to call the base class's version (for example, for a virtual `DoWrite()` persistence function).
- Functions in the Pimpl may require a "back pointer" to the visible object if they need to, in turn, use visible functions, which adds another level of indirection. (By convention, such a back pointer is usually named `self_` at PeerDirect.)
- Often the best compromise is to use Option 2, and in addition to put into `XImpl` only those non-private functions that need to be called by the private ones (see the back pointer comments below).

> **Guideline**
>
> *For widely used classes, prefer to use the compiler-firewall idiom (Pimpl Idiom) to hide implementation details. Use an opaque pointer (a pointer to a declared, but undefined, class) declared as "`struct XxxxImpl; XxxxImpl* pimpl_;`" to store private members (including both data and member functions).*

Option 3 (Score: 0 / 10): Put all private and protected members into `XImpl`. Taking this extra step to include protected members is actually wrong. Protected members should never go into a Pimpl, because putting them there just emasculates them. After all, pro-

4. Except in some liberal European countries.

tected members exist specifically to be seen and used by derived classes, so they aren't nearly as useful if derived classes can't see or use them.

Option 4 (Score: 10 / 10 in restricted cases): Make `XImpl` entirely the class that `X` would have been, and write X as only the public interface made up entirely of simple forwarding functions (another handle/body variant). This is useful in a few restricted cases and has the benefit of avoiding a back pointer, because all services are available within the Pimpl class. The chief drawback is that it usually makes the visible class useless for any inheritance as either a base or a derived class.

2. Does `XImpl` require a pointer back to the `X` object?

Does the Pimpl require a back pointer to the visible object? The answer is: Sometimes, unhappily, yes. After all, what we're doing is (somewhat artificially) splitting each object into two halves for the purposes of hiding one part.

Consider: Whenever a function in the visible class is called, usually some function or data in the hidden half is needed to complete the request. That's fine and reasonable. What's perhaps not as obvious at first is that often a function in the Pimpl must call a function in the visible class, usually because the called function is public or virtual. One way to minimize this is to use Option 4 (above) judiciously for the functions concerned—that is, implement Option 2 and, in addition, to put inside the Pimpl any nonprivate functions that are used by private functions.

Item 30: The "Fast Pimpl" Idiom — Difficulty: 6

It's sometimes tempting to cut corners in the name of "reducing dependencies" or in the name of "efficiency," but it may not always be a good idea. Here's an excellent idiom to accomplish both objectives simultaneously and safely.

Standard `malloc` and `new` calls are relatively expensive.[5] In the code below, the programmer originally has a data member of type `X` in class `Y`.

```
// Attempt #1
//
// file y.h
#include "x.h"
class Y
{
  /*...*/
  X x_;
};

// file y.cpp
Y::Y() {}
```

5. Compared with other typical operations, such as function calls.

This declaration of class Y requires the declaration of class X to be visible (from x.h). To avoid this, the programmer first tries to write:

```
// Attempt #2
//
// file y.h
class X;
class Y
{
  /*...*/
  X* px_;
};

// file y.cpp
#include "x.h"
Y::Y() : px_( new X ) {}
Y::~Y() { delete px_; px_ = 0; }
```

This nicely hides X, but it turns out that Y is used very widely and the dynamic allocation overhead is degrading performance.

Finally, our fearless programmer hits on the "perfect" solution that requires neither including x.h in y.h nor the inefficiency of dynamic allocation (and not even a forward declaration).

```
// Attempt #3
//
// file y.h
class Y
{
  /*...*/
  static const size_t sizeofx = /*some value*/;
  char x_[sizeofx];
};

// file y.cpp
#include "x.h"
Y::Y()
{
  assert( sizeofx >= sizeof(X) );
  new (&x_[0]) X;
}
Y::~Y()
{
  (reinterpret_cast<X*>(&x_[0]))->~X();
}
```

1. What is the Pimpl Idiom's space overhead?
2. What is the Pimpl Idiom's performance overhead?
3. Discuss Attempt #3. Can you think of a better way to get around the overhead?

Note: See Item 29 for more about the Pimpl Idiom.

Solution

Let's answer the Item questions one at a time.

1. What is the Pimpl Idiom's space overhead?

"What space overhead?" you ask? Well, we now need space for at least one extra pointer (and possibly two, if there's a back pointer in `XImpl`) for every `X` object. This typically adds at least 4 (or 8) bytes on many popular systems, and possibly as many as 14 bytes or more, depending on alignment requirements. For example, try the following program on your favorite compiler.

```
struct X { char c; struct XImpl; XImpl* pimpl_; };
struct X::XImpl { char c; };
int main()
{
  cout << sizeof(X::XImpl) << endl
       << sizeof(X) << endl;
}
```

On many popular compilers that use 32-bit pointers, this prints:

```
1
8
```

On these compilers, the overhead of storing one extra pointer was actually 7 bytes, not 4. Why? Because the platform on which the compiler is running requires a pointer to be stored on a 4-byte boundary, or else it performs much more poorly if the pointer isn't stored on such a boundary. Knowing this, the compiler allocates 3 bytes of unused/empty space inside each `X` object, which means the cost of adding a pointer member was actually 7 bytes, not 4. If a back pointer is also needed, then the total storage overhead can be as high as 14 bytes on a 32-bit machine, as high as 30 bytes on a 64-bit machine, and so on.

How do we get around this space overhead? The short answer is: We can't eliminate it, but sometimes we can minimize it.

The longer answer is: There's a downright reckless way to eliminate it that you should never, ever use (and don't tell anyone that you heard it from me), and there's usually a nonportable, but correct, way to minimize it. The utterly reckless "space optimization" happens to be the same as the utterly reckless "performance optimization," so I've moved that discussion off to the side; see the upcoming sidebox "Reckless Fixes and Optimizations, and Why They're Evil."

If (and only if) the space difference is actually important in your program, then the nonportable, but correct, way to minimize the pointer overhead is to use compiler-specific `#pragmas`. Many compilers will let you override the default alignment/packing for a given class; see your vendor's documentation for details. If your platform only "prefers" (rather than "enforces") pointer alignment and your compiler offers this feature, then on a 32-bit platform you can eliminate as much as 6 bytes of overhead per `X` object, at the (possibly minuscule) cost of run-time performance, because actually using the pointer will be slightly less efficient. Before you even consider anything like this, though, always follow the age-old sage advice: *First make it right, then make it fast*. Never optimize—neither for speed, nor for size—until your profiler and other tools tell you that you should.

2. What is the Pimpl Idiom's performance overhead?

Using the Pimpl idiom can have a performance overhead for two main reasons. For one thing, each `X` construction/destruction must now allocate/deallocate memory for its `XImpl` object, which is typically a relatively expensive operation.[6] For another, each access of a member in the Pimpl can require at least one extra indirection; if the hidden member being accessed itself uses a back pointer to call a function in the visible class, there will be multiple indirections.

How do we get around this performance overhead? The short answer is: Use the Fast Pimpl idiom, which I'll cover next. (There's also a downright reckless way to eliminate it that you should never, ever use; see the sidebar "Reckless Fixes and Optimizations, and Why They're Evil" for more information.)

3. Discuss Attempt #3.

The short answer about attempt #3 is: Don't do this. Bottom line, C++ doesn't support opaque types directly, and this is a brittle attempt (some people, like me, would even say "hack") to work around that limitation.

What the programmer almost certainly wants is something else, namely the Fast Pimpl idiom.

The second part of the third question was: Can you think of a better way to get around the overhead?

The main performance issue here is that space for the Pimpl objects is being allocated from the free store. In general, the right way to address allocation performance for a specific class is to provide a class-specific `operator new()` for that class and use a fixed-size allocator, because fixed-size allocators can be made much more efficient than general-purpose allocators.

```
// file x.h
class X
{
  /*...*/
  struct XImpl;
  XImpl* pimpl_;
};

// file x.cpp
#include "x.h"
```

6. Compared with most other common operations in C++, such as function calls. Note that here I'm specifically talking about the cost of using a general-purpose allocator, which is what you typically get with the builtin `::operator new()` and `malloc()`.

```
struct X::XImpl
{
  /*...private stuff here...*/
  static void* operator new( size_t )   { /*...*/ }
  static void  operator delete( void* ) { /*...*/ }
};
X::X() : pimpl_( new XImpl ) {}
X::~X() { delete pimpl_; pimpl_ = 0; }
```

"Aha!" you say. "We've found the holy grail—the Fast Pimpl!" you say. Well, yes, but hold on a minute and think about how this will work and what it will cost you.

Your favorite advanced C++ or general-purpose programming textbook has the details about how to write efficient fixed-size [de]allocation functions, so I won't cover that again here. I will talk about usability. One technique is to put the [de]allocation functions in a generic fixed-size allocator template, perhaps something like this:

```
template<size_t S>
class FixedAllocator
{
public:
  void* Allocate( /*requested size is always S*/ );
  void  Deallocate( void* );
private:
  /*...implemented using statics?...*/
};
```

Because the private details are likely to use statics, however, there could be problems if `Deallocate` is ever called from a static object's destructor. Probably safer is a singleton that manages a separate free list for each request size (or, as an efficiency tradeoff, a separate free list for each request size "bucket"—for example, one list for blocks of size 0-8, another for blocks of size 9-16, and so forth).

```
class FixedAllocator
{
public:
  static FixedAllocator& Instance();
  void* Allocate( size_t );
  void  Deallocate( void* );
private:
  /*...singleton implementation, typically
       with easier-to-manage statics than
       the templated alternative above...*/
};
```

Let's throw in a helper base class to encapsulate the calls. This works because derived classes "inherit" these overloaded base operators.

```
struct FastArenaObject
{
  static void* operator new( size_t s )
  {
    return FixedAllocator::Instance()->Allocate(s);
```

```
  }
  static void operator delete( void* p )
  {
    FixedAllocator::Instance()->Deallocate(p);
  }
};
```

Now, you can easily write as many Fast Pimpls as you like:

```
//  Want this one to be a Fast Pimpl?
//  Easy, then just inherit...
struct X::XImpl : FastArenaObject
{
  /*...private stuff here...*/
};
```

Applying this technique to the original problem, we get a variant of Attempt #2:

```
// file y.h

class X;
class Y
{
  /*...*/
  X* px_;
};

// file y.cpp

#include "x.h" // X now inherits from FastArenaObject
Y::Y() : px_( new X ) {}
Y::~Y() { delete px_; px_ = 0; }
```

But beware! This is nice, but don't use the Fast Pimpl willy nilly. You're getting extra allocation speed, but as usual you should never forget the cost. Managing separate free lists for objects of specific sizes usually means incurring a space efficiency penalty, because any free space is fragmented (more than usual) across several lists.

A final reminder: As with any other optimization, use Pimpls in general and Fast Pimpls in particular only after profiling and experience prove that the extra performance boost is really needed in your situation.

Guideline

Avoid inlining or detailed tuning until performance profiles prove the need.

Reckless Fixes and Optimizations, and Why They're Evil

The main solution text shows why using the Pimpl Idiom can incur space and performance overheads, and it also shows the right way to minimize or eliminate those overheads. There is also a sometimes-recommended, but wrong, way to deal with them.

Here's the reckless, unsafe, might-work-if-you're-lucky, evil, fattening, and high-cholesterol way to eliminate the space and performance overheads, and you didn't hear it from me—the only reason I'm mentioning it at all is because I've seen people try to do this:

```
// evil dastardly header file x.h
class X
{
  /* . . . */
  static const size_t sizeofximpl = /*some value*/;
  char pimpl_[sizeofximpl];
};

// pernicious depraved implementation file x.cpp
#include "x.h"
X::X()
{
  assert( sizeofximpl >= sizeof(XImpl) );
  new (&pimpl_[0]) XImpl;
}
X::~X()
{
  (reinterpret_cast<XImpl*>(&pimpl_[0]))->~XImpl();
}
```

DON'T DO THIS! Yes, it removes the space overhead—it doesn't use so much as a single pointer.[7] Yes, it removes the memory allocation overhead—there's nary a `malloc` or `new` in sight. Yes, it might even happen to work on the current version of your current compiler.

It's also completely nonportable. Worse, it will completely break your system, even if it does appear to work at first. Here are several reasons.

1. *Alignment*. Any memory that's allocated dynamically via `new` or `malloc` is guaranteed to be properly aligned for objects of any type, but buffers that are *not* allocated dynamically have no such guarantee:

```
char* buf1 = (char*)malloc( sizeof(Y) );
char* buf2 = new char[ sizeof(Y) ];
char  buf3[ sizeof(Y) ];
new (buf1) Y;     // OK, buf1 allocated dynamically (A)
new (buf2) Y;     // OK, buf2 allocated dynamically (B)
new (&buf3[0]) Y; // error, buf3 may not be suitably aligned
(reinterpret_cast<Y*>(buf1))->~Y(); // OK
(reinterpret_cast<Y*>(buf2))->~Y(); // OK
(reinterpret_cast<Y*>(&buf3[0]))->~Y(); // error
```

7. This completely hides the Pimpl class—but, of course, clients must still be recompiled if `sizeofximpl` changes.

Just to be clear: I'm not recommending that you do A or B. I'm just pointing out that they're legal, whereas the above attempt to have a Pimpl without dynamic allocation is not, even though it may (dangerously) appear to work correctly at first if you happen to get lucky.[8]

2. *Brittleness.* The author of `X` has to be inordinately careful with otherwise ordinary `X` functions. For example, `X` must not use the default assignment operator, but must either suppress assignment or supply its own. (Writing a safe `X::operator=()` isn't too hard, but I'll leave it as an exercise for the reader. Remember to account for exception safety in that and in `X::~X`.[9] Once you're finished, I think you'll agree that this is a lot more trouble than it's worth.)

3. *Maintenance cost.* When `sizeof(XImpl)` grows beyond `sizeofximpl`, the programmer must bump up `sizeofximpl`. This can be an unattractive maintenance burden. Choosing a larger value for `sizeofximpl` mitigates this, but at the expense of trading off efficiency (see #4).

4. *Inefficiency.* Whenever `sizeofximpl > sizeof(XImpl)`, space is being wasted. This can be minimized, but at the expense of maintenance effort (see #3).

5. *Just plain wrongheadedness.* In short, it's obvious that the programmer is trying to do "something unusual." Frankly, in my experience, "unusual" is just about always a synonym for "hack." Whenever you see this kind of subversion—whether it's allocating objects inside character arrays like this programmer is doing, or implementing an assignment using explicit destruction and placement as discussed in Item 41—you should Just Say No.

Bottom line, C++ doesn't support opaque types directly, and this is a brittle attempt to work around that limitation.

8. All right, I'll 'fess up: There actually is a (not very portable, but pretty safe) way to put the Pimpl class right into the main class like this, thus avoiding all space and time overhead. It involves creating a "`max_align`" struct that guarantees maximal alignment, and defining the Pimpl member as `union { max_align dummy; char pimpl_[sizeofximpl]; };`—this will guarantee sufficient alignment. For all the gory details, do a search for "`max_align`" on the Web or on DejaNews. However, I still strongly urge you not to go down this sordid path, because using a `max_align` solves only this first issue and does not address the second through fifth issues. You Have Been Warned.
9. See the Item 8 through 17 miniseries.

Name Lookup, Namespaces, and the Interface Principle

Item 31: Name Lookup and the Interface Principle—Part 1 Difficulty: $9\frac{1}{2}$

When you call a function, which function do you call? The answer is determined by name lookup, but you're almost certain to find some of the details surprising.

In the following code, which functions are called? Why? Analyze the implications.

```
namespace A
{
  struct X;
  struct Y;
  void f( int );
  void g( X );
}

namespace B
{
  void f( int i )
  {
    f( i );   // which f()?
  }

  void g( A::X x )
  {
    g( x );   // which g()?
  }

  void h( A::Y y )
  {
    h( y );   // which h()?
  }
}
```

Solution

Two of the three cases are (fairly) obvious, but the third requires a good knowledge of C++'s name lookup rules—in particular, Koenig lookup.

Let's start simple.

```
namespace A
{
  struct X;
  struct Y;
  void f( int );
  void g( X );
}
namespace B
{
  void f( int i )
  {
    f( i );   // which f()?
  }
```

This `f()` calls itself, with infinite recursion. The reason is that the only visible `f()` is `B::f()` itself.

There is another function with signature `f(int)`, namely the one in namespace `A`. If `B` had written "`using namespace A;`" or "`using A::f;`", then `A::f(int)` would have been visible as a candidate when looking up `f(int)`, and the `f(i)` call would have been ambiguous between `A::f(int)` and `B::f(int)`. Since `B` did not bring `A::f(int)` into scope, however, only `B::f(int)` can be considered, so the call unambiguously resolves to `B::f(int)`.

And now for a twist:

```
  void g( A::X x )
  {
    g( x );   // which g()?
  }
```

This call is ambiguous between `A::g(X)` and `B::g(X)`. The programmer must explicitly qualify the call with the appropriate namespace name to get the `g()` he wants.

You may at first wonder why this should be so. After all, as with `f()`, `B` hasn't written "`using`" anywhere to bring `A::g(X)` into its scope, so you'd think that only `B::g(X)` would be visible, right? Well, this would be true except for an extra rule that C++ uses when looking up names:

> Koenig Lookup[1] (simplified): *If you supply a function argument of class type (here `x`, of type `A::X`), then to look up the correct function name the compiler considers matching names in the namespace (here `A`) containing the argument's type.*

1. Named after Andrew Koenig, who nailed down its definition and is a long-time member of both AT&T's C++ team and the C++ standards committee. See also Koenig97.

There's a little more to it, but that's essentially it. Here's an example, right out of the standard.

```
namespace NS
{
  class T { };
  void f(T);
}
NS::T parm;
int main()
{
  f(parm);      // OK, calls NS::f
}
```

I won't delve here into the reasons why Koenig lookup is a Good Thing (if you want to stretch your imagination right now, take the above code and replace "NS" with "std", "T" with "string", and "f" with "operator<<" and consider the ramifications). See the next Item for much more on Koenig lookup and its implications for namespace isolation and for analyzing class dependencies.

Suffice it to say that Koenig lookup is, indeed, a Good Thing and that you should be aware of how it works, because it can sometimes affect the code you write.

Now back to a simple example:

```
  void h( A::Y y )
  {
    h( y );     // which h()?
  }
}
```

There is no other h(A::Y), so this h() calls itself with infinite recursion.

Although B::h()'s signature mentions a type found in namespace A, this doesn't affect name lookup because there are no functions in A matching the name and signature h(A::Y).

So, what does it mean? That brings us to the last part of our Item question: *Analyze the implications.*

In short, the meaning of code in namespace B is being affected by a function declared in the completely separate namespace A, even though B has done nothing but simply mention a type found in A and there's nary a "using" in sight.

What this means is that namespaces aren't quite as independent as people originally thought. Don't start denouncing namespaces just yet, though; namespaces are still pretty independent, and they fit their intended uses to a T. The purpose of this Item is just to point out one of the (rare) cases in which namespaces aren't quite hermetically sealed—and, in fact, in which they should *not* be hermetically sealed, as the following Item will show.

Item 32: Name Lookup and the Interface Principle—Part 2 Difficulty: 9

What's in a class? That is, what is "part of" a class and its interface?

Recall a traditional definition of a class:

> *A class describes a set of data, along with the functions that operate on that data.*

Our question is: What functions are "part of" a class, or make up the interface of a class?

Hint #1: Clearly nonstatic member functions are tightly coupled to the class, and public nonstatic member functions make up part of the class's interface. What about static member functions? What about free functions?

Hint #2: Take some time to consider the implications of Item 31.

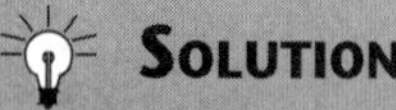

Solution

We'll start off with the deceptively simple question: *What functions are "part of" a class, or make up the interface of a class?*

The deeper questions are:

- How does this answer fit with C-style object-oriented programming?
- How does it fit with C++'s Koenig lookup? With the Myers Example? (I'll describe both.)
- How does it affect the way we analyze class dependencies and design object models?

So what's in a class? Here's the definition of "class" again:

> *A class describes a set of data, along with the functions that operate on that data.*

Programmers often unconsciously misinterpret this definition, saying instead: "Oh yeah, a class, that's what appears in the class definition—the member data and the member functions." But that's not the same thing, because it limits the word *functions* to mean just *member functions*. Consider:

```
//*** Example 1 (a)
class X { /*...*/ };
/*...*/
void f( const X& );
```

The question is: *Is* `f` *part of* `X`*?* Some people will automatically say "No" because `f` is a nonmember function (or free function). Others might realize something fundamentally important: If the Example 1 (a) code appears together in one header file, it is not significantly different from:

```
//*** Example 1 (b)
class X
{
  /*...*/
public:
  void f() const;
};
```

Think about this for a moment. Besides access rights,[2] `f` is still the same, taking a pointer/reference to `X`. The `this` parameter is just implicit in the second version, that's all. So, if Example 1 (a) all appears in the same header, we're already starting to see that even though `f` is not a member of `X`, it's nonetheless strongly related to `X`. I'll show exactly what that relationship is in the next section.

On the other hand, if `X` and `f` do not appear together in the same header file, then `f` is just some old client function, not a part of `X` (even if `f` is intended to augment `X`). We routinely write functions with parameters whose types come from library headers, and clearly our custom functions aren't part of those library classes.

With that example in mind, I propose the Interface Principle:

> *For a class X, all functions, including free functions, that both*
>
> - *"Mention" X*
> - *Are "supplied with" X*
>
> *are logically part of X, because they form part of the interface of X.*

By definition, every member function is "part of" `X`:

- Every member function must "mention" `X` (a nonstatic member function has an implicit `this` parameter of type `X* const` or `const X* const`; a static member function is in the scope of `X`).
- Every member function must be "supplied with" `X` (in `X`'s definition).

Applying the Interface Principle to Example 1 (a) gives the same result as our original analysis. Clearly, `f` mentions `X`. If `f` is also "supplied with" `X` (for example, if they come in the same header file and/or namespace[3]), then according to the Interface Principle, `f` is logically part of `X` because it forms part of the interface of `X`.

---

2. Even those may be unchanged if the original `f` was a friend.
3. We'll examine the relationship with namespaces in detail momentarily, because it turns out that this Interface Principle behaves in exactly the same way that Koenig lookup does.

So the Interface Principle is a useful touchstone to determine what is really "part of" a class. Do you find it unintuitive that a free function should be considered part of a class? Then let's give real weight to this example by giving a more common name to `f`.

```
//*** Example 1 (c)
class X { /*...*/ };
/*...*/
ostream& operator<<( ostream&, const X& );
```

Here the Interface Principle's rationale is perfectly clear, because we understand how this particular free function works. If `operator<<` is "supplied with" `X` (for example, in the same header and/or namespace), then `operator<<` is logically part of `X` because it forms part of the interface of `X`. That makes sense even though the function is a nonmember, because we know that it's common practice for a class's author to provide `operator<<`. If, instead, `operator<<` comes, not from `X`'s author, but from client code, then it's not part of `X` because it's not "supplied with" `X`.[4]

In this light, then, let's return to the traditional definition of a class:

> *A class describes a set of data, along with the functions that operate on that data.*

That definition is exactly right, for it doesn't say a thing about whether the "functions" in question are members or not.

I've been using C++ terms like "namespace" to describe what "supplied with" means, so is the Interface Principle C++-specific? Or is it a general OO principle that can apply in other languages?

Consider a familiar example from another (in fact, a non-OO) language.

```
/*** Example 2 (a) ***/
struct _iobuf { /*...data goes here...*/ };
typedef struct _iobuf FILE;
FILE* fopen ( const char* filename,
              const char* mode );
int   fclose( FILE* stream );
int   fseek ( FILE* stream,
              long  offset,
              int   origin );
long  ftell ( FILE* stream );
     /* etc. */
```

This is the standard "handle technique" for writing OO code in a language that doesn't have classes. You provide a structure that holds the object's data and functions—necessarily nonmembers—that take or return pointers to that structure. These free functions construct (`fopen`), destroy (`fclose`), and manipulate (`fseek`, `ftell`, and so forth) the data.

This technique has disadvantages (for example, it relies on client programmers to refrain from fiddling with the data directly), but it's still "real" OO code—after all, a class

4. The similarity between member and nonmember functions is even stronger for certain other overloadable operators. For example, when you write "`a+b`" you might be asking for `a.operator+(b)` or `operator+(a,b)`, depending on the types of `a` and `b`.

is "a set of data, along with the functions that operate on that data." In this case, of necessity, the functions are all nonmembers, but they are still part of the interface of `FILE`.

Now consider an "obvious" way to rewrite Example 2 (a) in a language that does have classes.

```
//*** Example 2 (b)
class FILE
{
public:
  FILE( const char* filename,
        const char* mode );
 ~FILE();
  int  fseek( long offset, int origin );
  long ftell();
       /* etc. */
private:
  /*...data goes here...*/
};
```

The `FILE*` parameters have just become implicit `this` parameters. Here it's clear that `fseek` is part of `FILE`, just as it was in Example 2 (a), even though there it was a nonmember. We can even merrily make some functions members and some not.

```
//*** Example 2 (c)
class FILE
{
public:
  FILE( const char* filename,
        const char* mode );
 ~FILE();
  long ftell();
       /* etc. */
private:
  /*...data goes here...*/
};
int fseek( FILE* stream,
           long  offset,
           int   origin );
```

It really doesn't matter whether the functions are members. As long as they "mention" `FILE` and are "supplied with" `FILE`, they really are part of `FILE`. In Example 2 (a), all the functions were nonmembers, because in C they have to be. Even in C++, some functions in a class's interface have to be (or should be) nonmembers. `operator<<` can't be a member, because it requires a stream as the left-hand argument, and `operator+` shouldn't be a member in order to allow conversions on the left-hand argument.

A Deeper Look at Koenig Lookup

The Interface Principle makes even more sense when you realize that it does exactly the same thing as Koenig lookup. I'll use two examples to illustrate and define Koenig lookup.

In the next section, I'll use the Myers Example to show why this is directly related to the Interface Principle.

Here's why we need Koenig lookup, using the same example as in Item 31. It's right out of the C++ standard.

```
//*** Example 3 (a)
namespace NS
{
  class T { };
  void f(T);
}
NS::T parm;
int main()
{
  f(parm);     // OK: calls NS::f
}
```

Pretty nifty, isn't it? "Obviously" the programmer shouldn't have to explicitly write `NS::f(parm)`, because just `f(parm)` "obviously" means `NS::f(parm)`, right? But what's obvious to us isn't always obvious to a compiler, especially considering there's nary a "`using`" in sight to bring the name `f` into scope. Koenig lookup lets the compiler do the right thing.

Here's how it works: Recall that "name lookup" just means that, whenever you write a call like "`f(parm)`", the compiler has to figure out which function named `f` you want. (With overloading and scoping, there could be several functions named `f`.) Koenig lookup says that, if you supply a function argument of class type (here `parm`, of type `NS::T`), then to find the function name the compiler is required to look, not just in the usual places, such as the local scope, but also in the namespace (here, `NS`) that contains the argument's type.[5] So Example 3 (a) works: The parameter being passed to `f` is a `T`, `T` is defined in namespace `NS`, and the compiler can consider the `f` in namespace `NS`—no fuss, no muss.

It's good that we don't have to explicitly qualify `f`, because sometimes we *can't* easily qualify a function name.

```
//*** Example 3 (b)
#include <iostream>
#include <string>  // this header declares the function
                   //   std::operator<< for strings
int main()
{
  std::string hello = "Hello, world";
  std::cout << hello;   // OK: calls std::operator<<
}
```

Here the compiler has no way to find `operator<<` without Koenig lookup, because the `operator<<` we want is a free function that's made known to us only as part of the `string` package. It would be disgraceful if the programmer were forced to qualify this function name, because then the last line couldn't use the operator naturally. Instead, we would have to write

5. There's a little more to the mechanics, but that's essentially it.

either "`std::operator<<( std::cout, hello );`" which is exceedingly ugly, or "`using std::operator<<;`" which is annoying and quickly becomes tedious if there are many operators, or "`using namespace std;`" which dumps all the names in `std` into the current namespace and thus eliminates much of the advantage of having namespaces in the first place. If those options send shivers down your spine, you understand why we need Koenig lookup.

In summary, if in the same namespace you supply a class and a free function that mentions that class,[6] the compiler will enforce a strong relationship between the two.[7] And that brings us back to the Interface Principle, because of the Myers Example.

More Koenig Lookup: The Myers Example

Consider first a (slightly) simplified example.

```
//*** Example 4 (a)
namespace NS    // this part is
{               // typically from
  class T { }; // some header
}               // file T.h
void f( NS::T );
int main()
{
  NS::T parm;
  f(parm);      // OK: calls global f
}
```

Namespace `NS` supplies a type `T`, and the outside code provides a global function `f` that happens to take a `T`. This is fine, the sky is blue, the world is at peace, and everything is wonderful.

Time passes. One fine day, the author of `NS` helpfully adds a function:

```
//*** Example 4 (b)
namespace NS    // typically from
{               // some header T.h
  class T { };
  void f( T ); // <-- new function
}
void f( NS::T );
int main()
{
  NS::T parm;
  f(parm);      // ambiguous: NS::f
}               //   or global f?
```

Adding a function in a namespace scope "broke" code outside the namespace, even though the client code didn't write `using` to bring `NS`'s names into its scope! But wait, it

6. By value, reference, pointer, or whatever.

7. Granted, that relationship is still less strong than the relationship between a class and one of its member functions. See *"How Strong Is the 'Part of' Relationship?"* later in this Item.

gets better—Nathan Myers pointed out the following interesting behavior with namespaces and Koenig lookup.

```
//*** The Myers Example: "Before"
namespace A
{
  class X { };
}
namespace B
{
  void f( A::X );
  void g( A::X parm )
  {
    f(parm);    // OK: calls B::f
  }
}
```

This is fine, the sky is blue. One fine day, the author of A helpfully adds another function.

```
//*** The Myers Example: "After"
namespace A
{
  class X { };
  void f( X ); // <-- new function
}
namespace B
{
  void f( A::X );
  void g( A::X parm )
  {
    f(parm);    // ambiguous: A::f or B::f?
  }
}
```

"Huh?" you might ask. "The whole point of namespaces is to prevent name collisions, isn't it? But adding a function in one namespace actually seems to 'break' code in a completely separate namespace." True, namespace B's code seems to break merely because it mentions a type from A. B's code didn't write a `using namespace A;` anywhere. It didn't even write `using A::X;`.

This is not a problem, and B is not broken. This is in fact *exactly* what should happen.[8] If there's a function `f(X)` in the same namespace as `X`, then, according to the Interface Principle, `f` is part of the interface of `X`. It doesn't matter a whit that `f` happens to be a free function; to see clearly that it's nonetheless logically part of `X`, just give it another name.

```
//*** Restating the Myers Example: "After"
namespace A
{
```

8. This very example arose at the Morristown meeting in November 1997, and it's what got me thinking about this issue of membership and dependencies.

How Strong Is the "Part of" Relationship?

While the Interface Principle states that both member and nonmember functions can be logically "part of" a class, it doesn't claim that members and nonmembers are equivalent. For example, member functions automatically have full access to class internals, whereas nonmembers have such access only if they're made friends. Likewise for name lookup, including Koenig lookup, the C++ language deliberately says that a member function is to be considered more strongly related to a class than a nonmember.

```
//*** NOT the Myers Example
namespace A
{
  class X { };
  void f( X );
}
class B      // <-- class, not namespace
{
  void f( A::X );
  void g( A::X parm )
  {
    f(parm); // OK: B::f, not ambiguous
  }
};
```

Now that we're talking about a `class B`, rather than a `namespace B`, there's no ambiguity. When the compiler finds a member named `f()`, it won't bother trying to use Koenig lookup to find free functions.

So in two major ways—access rules and lookup rules—even when a function is "part of" a class, according to the Interface Principle, a member is more strongly related to the class than a nonmember.

```
  class X { };
  ostream& operator<<( ostream&, const X& );
}
namespace B
{
  ostream& operator<<( ostream&, const A::X& );
  void g( A::X parm )
  {
    cout << parm; // ambiguous: A::operator<< or
  }               //   B::operator<<?
}
```

If client code supplies a function that mentions `X` and matches the signature of one provided in the same namespace as `X`, the call *should* be ambiguous. `B` *should* be forced to say which competing function it means, its own or that supplied with X. This is exactly what we should expect given the Interface Principle:

For a class X, all functions, including free functions, that both

- *"Mention" X*
- *Are "supplied with" X*

are logically part of X, because they form part of the interface of X.

What the Myers Example means is simply that namespaces aren't quite as independent as people originally thought, but they are still pretty independent and they fit their intended uses.

In short, it's no accident that the Interface Principle works exactly the same way as Koenig lookup. Koenig lookup works the way it does fundamentally *because* of the Interface Principle.

"How Strong Is the 'Part of' Relationship?" shows why a member function is still more strongly related to a class than a nonmember.

Item 33: Name Lookup and the Interface Principle—Part 3 Difficulty: 5

Take a few minutes to consider some implications of the Interface Principle on the way we reason about program design. We'll revisit a classic design problem: "What's the best way to write `operator<<()`?"

There are two main ways to write `operator<<()` for a class: as a free function that uses only the usual interface of the class (and possibly accessing nonpublic parts directly as a `friend`), or as a free function that calls a `virtual Print()` helper function in the class.

Which method is better? What are the tradeoffs?

Solution

Are you wondering why a question like this gets a title like "Name Lookup–Part 3"? If so, you'll soon see why, as we consider an application of the Interface Principle discussed in the previous Item.

What Does a Class Depend On?

"What's in a class?" isn't just a philosophical question. It's a fundamentally practical question, because without the correct answer, we can't properly analyze class dependencies.

To demonstrate this, consider a seemingly unrelated problem: *What's the best way to write* `operator<<` *for a class?* There are two main ways, both of which involve tradeoffs. I'll analyze both. In the end we'll find that we're back to the Interface Principle and that it has given us important guidance to analyze the tradeoffs correctly.

Here's the first way:

```
//*** Example 5 (a) -- nonvirtual streaming
class X
{
  /*...ostream is never mentioned here...*/
};
ostream& operator<<( ostream& o, const X& x )
{
  /* code to output an X to a stream */
  return o;
}
```

Here's the second:

```
//*** Example 5 (b) -- virtual streaming
class X
{
  /*...*/
public:
  virtual ostream& print( ostream& ) const;
};
ostream& X::print( ostream& o ) const
{
  /* code to output an X to a stream */
  return o;
}
ostream& operator<<( ostream& o, const X& x )
{
  return x.print( o );
}
```

Assume that in both cases the class and the function declaration appear in the same header and/or namespace. Which one would you choose? What are the tradeoffs? Historically, experienced C++ programmers have analyzed these options this way:

- Option (a)'s advantage *(we've said until now)* is that `X` has fewer dependencies. Because no member function of `X` mentions `ostream`, `X` does not *(appear to)* depend on `ostream`. Option (a) also avoids the overhead of an extra virtual function call.
- Option (b)'s advantage is that any `DerivedX` will also print correctly, even when an `X&` is passed to `operator<<`.

This is the traditional analysis. Alas, this analysis is flawed. Armed with the Interface Principle, we can see why: The first advantage in Option (a) is a phantom, as indicated by the comments in italics.

1. According to the Interface Principle, as long as `operator<<` both "mentions" X (true in both cases) and is "supplied with" X (true in both cases), it is logically part of `X`.

2. In both cases, `operator<<` mentions `ostream`, so `operator<<` depends on `ostream`.
3. Because, in both cases, `operator<<` is logically part of `X` and `operator<<` depends on `ostream`, therefore in both cases, `X` depends on `ostream`.

So what we've traditionally thought of as Option (a)'s main advantage is not an advantage at all. In both cases, `X` still in fact depends on `ostream` anyway. If, as is typical, `operator<<` and `X` appear in the same header `X.h`, then both `X`'s own implementation module and all client modules that use `X` physically depend on `ostream` and require at least its forward declaration in order to compile.

With Option (a)'s first advantage exposed as a phantom, the choice really boils down to just the virtual function call overhead. Without applying the Interface Principle, though, we would not have been able to as easily analyze the true dependencies (and therefore the true tradeoffs) in this common real-world example.

Bottom line, it's not always useful to distinguish between members and nonmembers, especially when it comes to analyzing dependencies, and that's exactly what the Interface Principle implies.

Some Interesting (and Even Surprising) Results

In general, if `A` and `B` are classes and `f(A,B)` is a free function:

- If `A` and `f` are supplied together, then `f` is part of `A`, so `A` depends on `B`.
- If `B` and `f` are supplied together, then `f` is part of `B`, so `B` depends on `A`.
- If `A`, `B`, and `f` are supplied together, then `f` is part of both `A` and `B`, so `A` and `B` are interdependent. This has long made sense on an instinctive level—if the library author supplies two classes and an operation that uses both, the three are probably intended to be used together. Now, however, the Interface Principle has given us a way to more clearly state this interdependency.

Finally, we get to the really interesting case. In general, if `A` and `B` are classes and `A::g(B)` is a member function of `A`:

- Because `A::g(B)` exists, clearly `A` always depends on `B`. No surprises so far.
- If `A` and `B` are supplied together, then of course `A::g(B)` and `B` are supplied together. Therefore, because `A::g(B)` both "mentions" `B` and is "supplied with" `B`, then according to the Interface Principle, it follows (perhaps surprisingly, at first) that `A::g(B)` is part of `B`, and because `A::g(B)` uses an (implicit) `A*` parameter, `B` depends on `A`. Because `A` also depends on `B`, this means that `A` and `B` are interdependent.

At first, it might seem like a stretch to consider a member function of one class as also part of another class, but this is true only if `A` and `B` are also *supplied together*. Consider: If `A` and `B` are supplied together (say, in the same header file) and `A` mentions `B` in a member function like this, "gut feel" already usually tells us `A` and `B` are probably interdependent. They are certainly strongly coupled and cohesive, and the fact that they are supplied together and interact means that: (a) they are intended to be used together, and (b) changes to one affect the other.

The problem is that, until now, it's been hard to prove A and B's interdependence with anything more substantial than gut feel. Now their interdependence can be demonstrated as a direct consequence of the Interface Principle.

Note that, unlike classes, namespaces don't need to be declared all at once, and what's "supplied together" depends on what parts of the namespace are visible.

```
//*** Example 6 (a)
//---file a.h---
namespace N { class B; } // forward decl
namespace N { class A; } // forward decl
class N::A { public: void g(B); };
//---file b.h---
namespace N { class B { /*...*/ }; }
```

Clients of A include a.h, so for them A and B are supplied together and are interdependent. Clients of B include b.h, so for them A and B are not supplied together.

In summary, I'd like you to take away three thoughts from this miniseries.

1. The Interface Principle: For a class X, all functions, including free functions, that both "mention" X and are "supplied with" X are logically part of X, because they form part of the interface of X.
2. Therefore, both member *and nonmember* functions can be logically "part of" a class. A member function is still more strongly related to a class than is a nonmember, however.
3. In the Interface Principle, a useful way to interpret "supplied with" is "appears in the same header and/or namespace." If the function appears in the same header as the class, it is "part of" the class in terms of dependencies. If the function appears in the same namespace as the class, it is "part of" the class in terms of object use and name lookup.

ITEM 34: NAME LOOKUP AND THE INTERFACE PRINCIPLE—PART 4 DIFFICULTY: 9

We conclude this miniseries by considering some implications of the Interface Principle on name lookup. Can you spot the (quite subtle) problem lurking in the following code?

1. What is name hiding? Show how it can affect the visibility of base class names in derived classes.
2. Will the following example compile correctly? Make your answer as complete as you can. Try to isolate and explain any areas of doubt.

```
// Example 2: Will this compile?
//
// In some library header:
namespace N { class C {}; }
int operator+(int i, N::C) { return i+1; }
```

```
// A mainline to exercise it:
#include <numeric>
int main()
{
  N::C a[10];
  std::accumulate(a, a+10, 0);
}
```

Solution

Let's recap a familiar inheritance issue: name hiding, by answering question 1 in the Item:

1. What is name hiding? Show how it can affect the visibility of base class names in derived classes.

Name Hiding

Consider the following example:

```
// Example 1a: Hiding a name
//             from a base class
//
struct B
{
  int f( int );
  int f( double );
  int g( int );
};
struct D : public B
{
private:
  int g( std::string, bool );
};
D   d;
int i;
d.f(i);  // ok, means B::f(int)
d.g(i);  // error: g takes 2 args
```

Most of us should be used to seeing this kind of name hiding, although the fact that the last line won't compile surprises most new C++ programmers. In short, when we declare a function named `g` in the derived class `D`, it automatically hides all functions with the same name in all direct and indirect base classes. It doesn't matter a whit that `D::g` "obviously" can't be the function that the programmer meant to call (not only does `D::g` have the wrong signature, but it's private and, therefore, inaccessible to boot), because `B::g` is hidden and can't be considered by name lookup.

To see what's really going on, let's look in a little more detail at what the compiler does when it encounters the function call `d.g(i)`. First, it looks in the immediate scope, in this case the scope of class `D`, and makes a list of all functions it can find that are named `g` (regardless of whether they're accessible or even take the right number of parameters). *Only if it doesn't find any at all* does it then continue "outward" into the next enclosing scope and repeat—in this case, the scope of the base class B—until it eventually either runs out of scopes without having found a function with the right name or else finds a scope that contains at least one candidate function. If a scope is found that has one or more candidate functions, the compiler then stops searching and works with the candidates that it's found, performing overload resolution and then applying access rules.

There are very good reasons why the language must work this way.[9] To take the extreme case, it makes intuitive sense that a member function that's a near-exact match ought to be preferred over a global function that would have been a perfect match had we considered the parameter types only.

How to Work Around Unwanted Name Hiding

Of course, there are the two usual ways around the name-hiding problem in Example 1a. First, the calling code can simply say which one it wants and force the compiler to look in the right scope.

```
// Example 1b: Asking for a name
//             from a base class
//
D   d;
int i;
d.f(i);     // ok, means B::f(int)
d.B::g(i); // ok, asks for B::g(int)
```

Second, and usually more appropriate, the designer of class D can make B::g visible with a using declaration. This allows the compiler to consider B::g in the same scope as D::g for the purposes of name lookup and subsequent overload resolution.

```
// Example 1c: Un-hiding a name
//             from a base class
//
struct D : public B
{
  using B::g;
private:
  int g( std::string, bool );
};
```

9. For example, one might think that if none of the functions found in an inner scope were usable, then it could be okay to let the compiler start searching further enclosing scopes. That would, however, produce surprising results in some cases (consider the case in which there's a function that would be an exact match in an outer scope, but there's a function in an inner scope that's a close match, requiring only a few parameter conversions). Or, one might think that the compiler should just make a list of all functions with the required name in all scopes and then perform overload resolution across scopes. But, alas, that too has its pitfalls (consider that a member function ought to be preferred over a global function, rather than result in a possible ambiguity).

Either of these gets around the hiding problem in the original Example 1a code.

Namespaces and the Interface Principle

Use namespaces wisely. If you put a class into a namespace, be sure to put all helper functions and operators into the same namespace too. If you don't, you may discover surprising effects in your code.

The following simple program is based on code e-mailed to me by astute reader Darin Adler. It supplies a class `C` in namespace `N` and an operation on that class. Notice that the `operator+()` is in the global namespace, not in namespace `N`. Does that matter? Isn't the code valid as written anyway?

Question 2, you will remember, was:

2. Will the following example compile correctly? Make your answer as complete as you can. Try to isolate and explain any areas of doubt.

```
// Example 2: Will this compile?
//
// In some library header:
namespace N { class C {}; }
int operator+(int i, N::C) { return i+1; }
// A mainline to exercise it:
#include <numeric>
int main()
{
  N::C a[10];
  std::accumulate(a, a+10, 0);
}
```

Before reading on, stop and consider the hints I've dropped so far: Will this program compile?[10] Is it portable?

Name Hiding in Nested Namespaces

Well, at first glance, Example 2 sure looks legal. So the answer is probably surprising: Maybe it will compile, maybe not. It depends entirely on your implementation, and I know of standard-conforming implementations that will compile this program correctly and equally standard-conforming implementations that won't. Gather 'round, and I'll show you why.

10. In case you're wondering that there might be a potential portability problem depending on whether the implementation of `std::accumulate()` invokes `operator+(int,N::C)` or `operator+(N::C,int)`, there isn't. The standard says that it must be the former, so Example 1 is providing an `operator+()` with the correct signature.

The key to understanding the answer is understanding what the compiler has to do inside `std::accumulate`. The `std::accumulate` template looks something like this:

```
namespace std
{
  template<class Iter, class T>
  inline T accumulate( Iter first,
                       Iter last,
                       T    value )
  {
    while( first != last )
    {
      value = value + *first;  // 1
      ++first;
    }
    return value;
  }
}
```

The code in Example 2 actually calls `std::accumulate<N::C*,int>`. In line 1 above, how should the compiler interpret the expression `value + *first`? Well, it's got to look for an `operator+()` that takes an `int` and an `N::C` (or parameters that can be converted to `int` and `N::C`). Hey, it just so happens that we have just such an `operator+(int,N::C)` at global scope! Look, there it is! Cool. So everything must be fine, right?

The problem is that the compiler may or may not be able to see the `operator+(int,N::C)` at global scope, depending on what other functions have already been seen to be declared in namespace `std` at the point where `std::accumulate<N::C*,int>` is instantiated.

To see why, consider that the same name hiding we observed with derived classes happens with any nested scopes, including namespaces, and consider *where* the compiler starts looking for a suitable `operator+()`. (Now I'm going to reuse my explanation from the earlier section, only with a few names substituted.) First, it looks in the immediate scope, in this case the scope of namespace `std`, and makes a list of all functions it can find that are named `operator+()` (regardless of whether they're accessible or even take the right number of parameters). *Only if it doesn't find any at all* does it then continue "outward" into the next enclosing scope and repeat—in this case, the scope of the next enclosing namespace outside `std`, which happens to be the global scope—until it eventually either runs out of scopes, without having found a function with the right name, or else finds a scope that contains at least one candidate function. If a scope is found that has one or more candidate functions, the compiler then stops searching and works with the candidates it's found, performing overload resolution and applying access rules.

In short, whether Example 2 will compile depends entirely on whether this implementation's version of the standard header `numeric`: a) declares an `operator+()` (any `operator+()`, suitable or not, accessible or not); or b) includes any other standard header that does so. Unlike standard C, standard C++ does not specify which standard headers will include each other, so when you include `numeric`, you may or may not get header `iterator` too, for example, which does define several `operator+()` functions. I know of C++ products that won't compile Example 2, others that will compile Example 2 but balk once you add the line `#include <vector>`, and so on.

Some Fun with Compilers

It's bad enough that the compiler can't find the right function if there happens to be another `operator+()` in the way, but typically the `operator+()` that does get encountered in a standard header is a template, and compilers generate notoriously difficult-to-read error messages when templates are involved. For example, one popular implementation reports the following errors when compiling Example 2 (note that in this implementation, the header `numeric` does in fact include the header `iterator`).

```
error C2784: 'class std::reverse_iterator<'template-parameter-
1','template-parameter-2','template-parameter-3','template-
parameter-4','template-parameter-5'> __cdecl std::operator
+(template-parameter-5,const class
std::reverse_iterator<'template-parameter-1','template-parameter-
2','template-parameter-3','template-parameter-4','template-
parameter-5'>&)' : could not deduce template argument for
'template-parameter-5' from 'int'

error C2677: binary '+' : no global operator defined which takes
type 'class N::C' (or there is no acceptable conversion)
```

Yikes! Imagine the poor programmer's confusion.

- The first error message is unreadable. The compiler is merely complaining (as clearly as it can) that it did find an `operator+()` but can't figure out how to use it in an appropriate way. But that doesn't help the poor programmer. "Huh?" saith the programmer, scratching at his scalp beneath his forelock, "when did I ever ask for a `reverse_iterator` anywhere?"
- The second message is a flagrant lie, and it's the compiler vendor's fault (although perhaps an understandable mistake, because the message was probably right in most of the cases in which it came up before people began to use namespaces widely). It's close to the correct message "no operator *found* which takes...," but that doesn't help the poor programmer either. "Huh?" saith the programmer, now indignant with ire, "there is too a global operator defined that takes type `'class N::C'`!"

How is a mortal programmer ever to decipher what's going wrong here? And, once he does, how loudly is he likely to curse the author of class `N::C`? Best to avoid the problem completely, as we shall now see.

The Solution

When we encountered this problem in the familiar guise of base/derived name hiding, we had two possible solutions: Have the calling code explicitly say which function it wants (Example 1b), or write a `using` declaration to make the desired function visible in the right scope (Example 1c). Neither solution works in this case. The first is possible[11] but places an unacceptable burden on the programmer; the second is impossible.

The real solution is to put our `operator+()` where it has always truly belonged and where it should have been put in the first place: in namespace `N`.

```
// Example 2b: Solution
//
// in some library header
namespace N
{
  class C {};
  int operator+(int i, N::C) { return i+1; }
}
// a mainline to exercise it
#include <numeric>
int main()
{
  N::C a[10];
  std::accumulate(a, a+10, 0);// now ok
}
```

This code is portable and will compile on all conforming compilers, regardless of what happens to be already defined in `std` or any other namespace. Now that the `operator+()` is in the same namespace as the second parameter, when the compiler tries to resolve the "+" call inside `std::accumulate`, it is able to see the right `operator+()` because of Koenig lookup. Recall that Koenig lookup says that, in addition to looking in all the usual scopes, the compiler shall also look in the scopes of the function's parameter types to see if it can find a match. `N::C` is in namespace `N`, so the compiler looks in namespace `N`, and happily finds exactly what it needs, no matter how many other `operator+()`'s happen to be lying around and cluttering up namespace `std`.

The conclusion is that the problem arose because Example 2 did not follow the Interface Principle:

For a class X, all functions, including free functions, that both

- *"Mention" X*
- *Are "supplied with" X*

are logically part of X, because they form part of the interface of X.

If an operation, even a free function (and especially an operator) mentions a class and is intended to form part of the interface of a class, then always be sure to supply it with the class—which means, among other things, to put it in the same namespace as the class. The problem in Example 2 arose because we wrote a class `C` *and put part of its interface in a different namespace*. Making sure that the class and the interface stay together is The

11. By requiring the programmer to use the version of `std::accumulate` that takes a predicate and explicitly say which one he wants each time…a good way to lose customers.

Right Thing to Do in any case, and is a simple way of avoiding complex name lookup problems later on, when other people try to use your class.

Use namespaces wisely. Either put all of a class inside the same namespace—including things that to innocent eyes don't look like they're part of the class, such as free functions that mention the class (don't forget the Interface Principle)—or don't put the class in a namespace at all. Your users will thank you.

Guideline

Use namespaces wisely. If you write a class in some namespace `N`*, be sure to put all helper functions and operators into* `N`*, too. If you don't, you may discover surprising effects in your code.*

Memory Management

Item 35: Memory Management—Part 1 Difficulty: 3

How well do you know memory? What different memory areas are there?

This problem covers basics about C++'s main distinct memory stores. The following problem goes on to attack some deeper memory management questions in more detail.

C++ has several distinct memory areas in which objects and nonobject values may be stored, and each area has different characteristics.

Name as many of the distinct memory areas as you can. For each, summarize its performance characteristics and describe the lifetime of objects stored there.

Example: The stack stores automatic variables, including both builtins and objects of class type.

Solution

The following table summarizes a C++ program's major distinct memory areas. Note that some of the names (for example, "heap") do not appear as such in the standard; in particular, "heap" and "free store" are common and convenient shorthands for distinguishing between two kinds of dynamically allocated memory.

Table 1: C++'s Memory Areas

Memory Area	Characteristics and Object Lifetimes
Const Data	The const data area stores string literals and other data whose values are known at compile-time. No objects of class type can exist in this area. All data in this area is available during the entire lifetime of the program. Further, all this data is read-only, and the results of trying to modify it are undefined. This is in part because even the underlying storage format is subject to arbitrary optimization by the implementation. For example, a particular compiler may choose to store string literals in overlapping objects as an optional optimization.
Stack	The stack stores automatic variables. Objects are constructed immediately at the point of definition and destroyed immediately at the end of the same scope, so there is no opportunity for programmers to directly manipulate allocated but uninitialized stack space (barring willful tampering using explicit destructors and placement `new`). Stack memory allocation is typically much faster than for dynamic storage (heap or free store) because each stack memory allocation involves only a stack pointer increment rather than more-complex management.
Free Store	The free store is one of the two dynamic memory areas allocated/freed by `new`/`delete`. Object lifetime can be less than the time the storage is allocated. That is, free store objects can have memory allocated, without being immediately initialized, and they can be destroyed, without the memory being immediately deallocated. During the period when the storage is allocated but outside the object's lifetime, the storage may be accessed and manipulated through a `void*`, but none of the proto-object's nonstatic members or member functions may be accessed, have their addresses taken, or be otherwise manipulated.
Heap	The heap is the other dynamic memory area allocated/freed by `malloc()`/`free()` and their variants. Note that while the default global operators `new` and `delete` might be implemented in terms of `malloc()` and `free()` by a particular compiler, the heap is not the same as free store, and memory allocated in one area cannot be safely deallocated in the other. Memory allocated from the heap can be used for objects of class type by placement `new` construction and explicit destruction. If so used, the notes about free store object lifetime apply similarly here.
Global/Static	Global or static variables and objects have their storage allocated at program startup, but may not be initialized until after the program has begun executing. For instance, a static variable in a function is initialized only the first time program execution passes through its definition. The order of initialization of global variables across translation units is not defined, and special care is needed to manage dependencies between global objects (including class statics). As always, uninitialized proto-objects' storage may be accessed and manipulated through a `void*`, but no nonstatic members or member functions may be used or referenced outside the object's actual lifetime.

It's important to distinguish between the "heap" and the "free store," because the standard deliberately leaves unspecified the question of whether these two areas are related. For example, when memory is deallocated via `::operator delete()`, the final note in section 18.4.1.1 of the C++ standard states:

> *"It is unspecified under what conditions part or all of such reclaimed storage is allocated by a subsequent call to* `operator new` *or any of* `calloc`, `malloc`, *or* `realloc`, *declared in* `<cstdlib>`*."*

Further, it is unspecified whether `new`/`delete` is implemented in terms of `malloc`/`free` in a given implementation. It is specified, however, that `malloc`/`free` must *not* be implemented in terms of `new`/`delete`, according to 20.4.6, paragraphs 3 and 4:

> *"The functions* `calloc()`, `malloc()`, *and* `realloc()` *do not attempt to allocate storage by calling* `::operator new()`.
>
> *"The function* `free()` *does not attempt to deallocate storage by calling* `::operator delete()`*."*

Effectively, the heap and the free store behave differently and are accessed differently, so be sure to use them differently.

Guideline

Understand the five major distinct memory stores, why they're different, and how they behave: stack (automatic variables); free store (`new`/`delete`*); heap (*`malloc`/`free`*); global scope (statics, global variables, file scope variables, and so forth); const data (string literals, and so forth).*

Guideline

Prefer using the free store (`new`/`delete`*). Avoid using the heap (*`malloc`/`free`*).*

Item 36: Memory Management—Part 2 Difficulty: 6

Are you thinking about doing your own class-specific memory management, or even replacing C++'s global `new` *and* `delete`*? First, try this problem on for size.*

The following code shows classes that perform their own memory management. Point out as many memory-related errors as possible, and answer the additional questions.

1. Consider the following code:

```
class B
{
public:
  virtual ~B();
  void operator delete  ( void*, size_t ) throw();
  void operator delete[]( void*, size_t ) throw();
  void f( void*, size_t ) throw();
};
class D : public B
{
public:
  void operator delete  ( void* ) throw();
  void operator delete[]( void* ) throw();
};
```

Why do `B`'s operators `delete` have a second parameter, whereas `D`'s do not? Do you see any way to improve the function declarations?

2. Continuing with the same piece of code: Which `operator delete()` is called for each of the following `delete` expressions? Why, and with what parameters?

```
D* pd1 = new D;
delete pd1;
B* pb1 = new D;
delete pb1;
D* pd2 = new D[10];
delete[] pd2;
B* pb2 = new D[10];
delete[] pb2;
```

3. Are the following two assignments legal?

```
typedef void (B::*PMF)(void*, size_t);
PMF p1 = &B::f;
PMF p2 = &B::operator delete;
```

4. Are there any memory-related errors or issues in the following code?

```
class X
{
public:
  void* operator new( size_t s, int )
                   throw( bad_alloc )
  {
    return ::operator new( s );
  }
};
class SharedMemory
{
public:
  static void* Allocate( size_t s )
  {
    return OsSpecificSharedMemAllocation( s );
  }
  static void  Deallocate( void* p, int i = 0 )
  {
    OsSpecificSharedMemDeallocation( p, i );
  }
};
class Y
{
public:
  void* operator new( size_t s,
                      SharedMemory& m ) throw( bad_alloc )
  {
    return m.Allocate( s );
  }
  void  operator delete( void* p,
                         SharedMemory& m,
                         int i ) throw()
  {
     m.Deallocate( p, i );
  }
};
void operator delete( void* p ) throw()
{
  SharedMemory::Deallocate( p );
}
void operator delete( void* p,
                      std::nothrow_t& ) throw()
{
  SharedMemory::Deallocate( p );
}
```

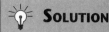

Solution

Let's take the questions one at a time.

1. Consider the following code:

```
class B
{
public:
  virtual ~B();
  void operator delete  ( void*, size_t ) throw();
  void operator delete[]( void*, size_t ) throw();
  void f( void*, size_t ) throw();
};

class D : public B
{
public:
  void operator delete  ( void* ) throw();
  void operator delete[]( void* ) throw();
};
```

Why do `B`'s operators `delete` have a second parameter, whereas `D`'s do not?

The answer is: It's just preference, that's all. Both are usual deallocation functions, not placement `delete`s. (For those keeping score at home, see section 3.7.3.2/2 in the C++ standard.)

However, there's also a memory error lurking in this underbrush. Both classes provide an `operator delete()` and `operator delete[]()`, without providing the corresponding `operator new()` and `operator new[]()`. This is extremely dangerous, because the default `operator new()` and `operator new[]()` are unlikely to do the right thing. (For example, consider what happens if a further-derived class provides its own `operator new()` or `operator new[]()` functions.)

Guideline

Always provide both class-specific `new` (or `new[]`) and class-specific `delete` (or `delete[]`) if you provide either.

And the second part of the question: Do you see any way to improve the function declarations?

All flavors of `operator new()` and `operator delete()` are always static functions, even if they're not declared `static`. Although C++ doesn't force you to say "`static`" explicitly when you declare your own, it's better to do so anyway, because it serves as a reminder to yourself as you're writing the code and as a reminder to the next programmer who has to maintain it.

Guideline

Always explicitly declare `operator new()` and `operator delete()` as static functions. They are never nonstatic member functions.

2. Continuing with the same piece of code: Which `operator delete()` is called for each of the following `delete` expressions? Why, and with what parameters?

```
D* pd1 = new D;
delete pd1;
```

This calls `D::operator delete(void*)`.

```
B* pb1 = new D;
delete pb1;
```

This also calls `D::operator delete(void*)`. Since `B`'s destructor is virtual, of course `D`'s destructor is properly called, but the fact that `B`'s destructor is virtual also implicitly means that `D::operator delete()` must be called, even though `B::operator delete()` is not (in fact, cannot be) virtual.

As an aside to those who are interested in how compilers implement these things: The usual method is that the code actually generated for every destructor is given an invisible "when done destroying the object, should I delete it?" flag that is set appropriately (`false` when destroying an automatic object, `true` when destroying a dynamic object). The last thing the generated destructor code does is check the flag and, if it's `true`, call the correct `operator delete()`.[1] This technique automatically ensures the correct behavior, namely that `operator delete()` appears to act "virtually" even though it is a static function and, therefore, cannot be virtual.

```
D* pd2 = new D[10];
delete[] pd2;
```

This calls `D::operator delete[](void*)`.

```
B* pb2 = new D[10];
delete[] pb2;
```

This is undefined behavior. The language requires that the static type of the pointer that is passed to `operator delete[]()` must be the same as its dynamic type. For more information on this topic, see also Scott Meyers' section, "Never Treat Arrays Polymorphically" in Meyers99.

Guideline

Never treat arrays polymorphically.

1. The correct variant techniques for array-delete operations are left as an exercise for the reader.

Guideline

Prefer using `vector<>` *or* `deque<>` *instead of arrays.*

3. Are the following two assignments legal?

```
typedef void (B::*PMF)(void*, size_t);
PMF p1 = &B::f;
PMF p2 = &B::operator delete;
```

The first assignment is fine; we're simply assigning the address of a member function to a pointer to member function.

The second assignment is illegal because `void operator delete( void*, size_t ) throw()` is *not* a nonstatic member function of `B`, even though as it's written, it may look like one. The trick here is to remember that `operator new()` and `operator delete()` are always static members, even if they're not explicitly declared static. It's a good habit to always declare them static, just to make sure that the fact is obvious to all programmers reading through your code.

Guideline

Always explicitly declare `operator new()` *and* `operator delete()` *as static functions. They are never nonstatic member functions.*

4. Are there any memory-related errors or issues in the following code?

Short answer: Yes, in every case. Some of them are just a little more subtle than others, that's all.

```
class X
{
public:
  void* operator new( size_t s, int )
                      throw( bad_alloc )
  {
    return ::operator new( s );
  }
};
```

This invites a memory leak, because no corresponding placement `delete` exists. Similarly below:

```
class SharedMemory
{
public:
  static void* Allocate( size_t s )
  {
    return OsSpecificSharedMemAllocation( s );
  }
```

```
    static void  Deallocate( void* p, int i )
    {
      OsSpecificSharedMemDeallocation( p, i );
    }
  };
  class Y
  {
  public:
    void* operator new( size_t s,
                        SharedMemory& m ) throw( bad_alloc )
    {
      return m.Allocate( s );
    }
```

This invites a memory leak, because no `operator delete()` matches this signature. If an exception is thrown during construction of an object to be located in memory allocated by this function, the memory will not be properly freed. For example, consider the following code:

```
SharedMemory shared;
...
new (shared) Y; // if Y::Y() throws, memory is leaked
```

Further, any memory allocated by this `operator new()` cannot safely be deleted because the class does not provide a usual `operator delete()`. This means that a base or derived class's `operator delete()`, or the global one, will have to try to deal with this deallocation (almost certainly unsuccessfully, unless you also replace all such surrounding `operator delete`'s, which would be onerous and evil).

```
    void  operator delete( void* p,
                           SharedMemory& m,
                           int i ) throw()
    {
      m.Deallocate( p, i );
    }
  };
```

This `Y::operator delete()` is useless because it can never be called.

```
  void operator delete( void* p )  throw()
  {
    SharedMemory::Deallocate( p );
  }
```

This is a serious error, because the replacement global `operator delete()` is going to delete memory allocated normally by the default `::operator new()`, not by `SharedMemory::Allocate()`. The best you can hope for is a quick core dump. Evil.

```
void operator delete( void* p,
                      std::nothrow_t& ) throw()
{
  SharedMemory::Deallocate( p );
}
```

The same comment applies again here, but this time it's slightly more subtle. This replacement `operator delete()` will be called only if an expression like "`new (nothrow) T`" fails because `T`'s constructor exits with an exception and will try to deallocate memory not allocated by `SharedMemory::Allocate()`. Evil and insidious.

> **Guideline**
>
> *Always provide both class-specific* `new` *(or* `new[]`*) and class-specific* `delete` *(or* `delete[]`*) if you provide either.*

If you got and understood all of these answers, then you're definitely on your way to becoming an expert in memory-management mechanics.

ITEM 37: AUTO_PTR — DIFFICULTY: 8

This Item covers basics about how you can use the standard `auto_ptr` *safely and effectively.*

Historical note: The original simpler form of this Item, appearing as a Special Edition of *Guru of the Week,* was first published in honor of the voting out of the *Final Draft International Standard for Programming Language C++*. It was known/suspected that `auto_ptr` would change one last time at the final meeting, where the standard was to be voted complete (Morristown, New Jersey, November 1997), so this problem was posted the day before the meeting began. The solution, freshly updated to reflect the prior day's changes to the standard, became the first published treatment of the standard `auto_ptr`.

Many thanks from all of us to Bill Gibbons, Greg Colvin, Steve Rumsby, and others who worked hard on the final refinement of `auto_ptr`. Greg, in particular, has labored over `auto_ptr` and related smart pointer classes for many years to satisfy various committee concerns and requirements, and deserves public recognition for that work.

This problem, now with a considerably more comprehensive and refined solution, illustrates the reasons for the eleventh-hour changes that were made, and it shows how you can make the best possible use of `auto_ptr`.

Comment on the following code: What's good, what's safe, what's legal, and what's not?

```
auto_ptr<T> source()
{
  return auto_ptr<T>( new T(1) );
}
void sink( auto_ptr<T> pt ) { }
void f()
{
  auto_ptr<T> a( source() );
  sink( source() );
  sink( auto_ptr<T>( new T(1) ) );
```

```
    vector< auto_ptr<T> > v;
    v.push_back( auto_ptr<T>( new T(3) ) );
    v.push_back( auto_ptr<T>( new T(4) ) );
    v.push_back( auto_ptr<T>( new T(1) ) );
    v.push_back( a );
    v.push_back( auto_ptr<T>( new T(2) ) );
    sort( v.begin(), v.end() );
    cout << a->Value();
  }
  class C
  {
  public:    /*...*/
  protected: /*...*/
  private:   /*...*/
    auto_ptr<CImpl> pimpl_;
  };
```

Solution

Most people have heard of the standard auto_ptr smart pointer facility, but not everyone uses it daily. That's a shame, because it turns out that auto_ptr neatly solves common C++ coding problems, and using it well can lead to more-robust code. This article shows how to use auto_ptr correctly to make your code safer—and how to avoid the dangerous but common abuses of auto_ptr that create intermittent and hard-to-diagnose bugs.

Why "Auto" Pointer?

auto_ptr is just one of a wide array of possible smart pointers. Many commercial libraries provide more-sophisticated kinds of smart pointers that can do wild and wonderful things, from managing reference counts to providing advanced proxy services. Think of the standard C++ auto_ptr as the Ford Escort of smart pointers—a simple, general-purpose smart pointer that doesn't have all the gizmos and luxuries of special-purpose or high-performance smart pointers, but does many common things well and is perfectly suitable for regular use.

What auto_ptr does is own a dynamically allocated object and perform automatic cleanup when the object is no longer needed. Here's a simple example of code that's unsafe without auto_ptr.

```
// Example 1(a): Original code
//
void f()
{
  T* pt( new T );
  /*...more code...*/
  delete pt;
}
```

Most of us write code like this every day. If f() is a three-line function that doesn't do anything exceptional, this may be fine. But if f() never executes the delete statement, either because of an early return or because of an exception thrown during execution of the function body, then the allocated object is not deleted and we have a classic memory leak.

A simple way to make Example 1(a) safe is to wrap the pointer in a "smarter," pointer-like object that owns the pointer and that, when destroyed, deletes the pointed-at object automatically. Because this smart pointer is simply used as an automatic object (that is, one that's destroyed automatically when it goes out of scope), it's reasonably called an "auto" pointer:

```
// Example 1(b): Safe code, with auto_ptr
//
void f()
{
  auto_ptr<T> pt( new T );
  /*...more code...*/
} // cool: pt's destructor is called as it goes out
  // of scope, and the object is deleted automatically
```

Now the code will not leak the T object, no matter whether the function exits normally or by means of an exception, because pt's destructor will always be called during stack unwinding. The cleanup happens automatically.

Finally, using an auto_ptr is just about as easy as using a builtin pointer, and to "take back" the resource and assume manual ownership again, we just call release().

```
// Example 2: Using an auto_ptr
//
void g()
{
  T* pt1 = new T;
  // right now, we own the allocated object
  // pass ownership to an auto_ptr
  auto_ptr<T> pt2( pt1 );
  // use the auto_ptr the same way
  // we'd use a simple pointer
  *pt2 = 12;        // same as "*pt1 = 12;"
  pt2->SomeFunc(); // same as "pt1->SomeFunc();"
  // use get() to see the pointer value
  assert( pt1 == pt2.get() );
  // use release() to take back ownership
  T* pt3 = pt2.release();
  // delete the object ourselves, since now
  // no auto_ptr owns it any more
  delete pt3;
} // pt2 doesn't own any pointer, and so won't
  // try to delete it... OK, no double delete
```

Finally, we can use auto_ptr's reset() function to reset the auto_ptr to own a different object. If the auto_ptr already owns an object, though, it first deletes the already-owned object, so calling reset() is much the same as destroying the auto_ptr and creating a new one that owns the new object.

```
// Example 3: Using reset()
//
void h()
{
  auto_ptr<T> pt( new T(1) );
  pt.reset( new T(2) );
    // deletes the first T that was
    // allocated with "new T(1)"
} // finally, pt goes out of scope and
  // the second T is also deleted
```

Wrapping Pointer Data Members

Similarly, auto_ptr can be used to safely wrap pointer data members. Consider the following common example that uses the Pimpl (or compiler-firewall) Idiom.[2]

```
// Example 4(a): A typical Pimpl
//

// file c.h
//
class C
{
public:
  C();
  ~C();
  /*...*/
private:
  struct CImpl; // forward declaration
  CImpl* pimpl_;
};

// file c.cpp
//
struct C::CImpl { /*...*/ };
C::C() : pimpl_( new CImpl ) { }
C::~C() { delete pimpl_; }
```

In brief, C's private details are split off into a separate implementation object that's hidden behind an opaque pointer. The idea is that C's constructor is responsible for allocating the private helper Pimpl object that contains the class's hidden internals, and C's

2. The Pimpl Idiom is useful for reducing project build times because it prevents wide-ranging recompilations of client code whenever the private portions of C change. For more about the Pimpl Idiom and how best to deploy compiler firewalls, see Items 26 through 30.

destructor is responsible for deallocating it. Using auto_ptr, however, we find an easier way:

```
// Example 4(b): A safer Pimpl, using auto_ptr
//
// file c.h
//
class C
{
public:
  C();
  ~C();
  /*...*/
private:
  struct CImpl; // forward declaration
  auto_ptr<CImpl> pimpl_;
  C& operator = ( const C& );
  C( const C& );
};
// file c.cpp
//
struct C::CImpl { /*...*/ };
C::C() : pimpl_( new CImpl ) { }
C::~C() {}
```

Now the destructor doesn't need to worry about deleting the pimpl_ pointer, because the auto_ptr will handle it automatically. Better still, it means C::C() has to do less work to detect and recover from constructor failures because pimpl_ is always automatically cleaned up. This can be easier than managing the pointer manually, and it follows the good practice of wrapping resource ownership in objects—a job that auto_ptr is well suited to do. We'll revisit this example again at the end.

Ownership, Sources, and Sinks

This is nifty stuff all by itself, but it gets better. It's also very useful to pass auto_ptrs to and from functions, as function parameters and return values.

To see why, first consider what happens when you copy an auto_ptr: An auto_ptr owns the object that it holds a pointer to, and only one auto_ptr may own an object at a time. When you copy an auto_ptr, you automatically transfer ownership from the source auto_ptr to the target auto_ptr; if the target auto_ptr already owns an object, that object is first freed. After the copy, only the target auto_ptr owns the pointer and will delete it in due time, while the source is set back to a null state and can no longer be used to refer to the owned object.

For example:

```
// Example 5: Transferring ownership from
//            one auto_ptr to another
//
void f()
{
  auto_ptr<T> pt1( new T );
  auto_ptr<T> pt2;
```

```
    pt1->DoSomething(); // OK
    pt2 = pt1;  // now pt2 owns the pointer,
                // and pt1 does not
    pt2->DoSomething(); // OK
  } // as we go out of scope, pt2's destructor
    // deletes the pointer, but pt1's does nothing
```

But be careful to avoid the pitfall of trying to use a nonowning `auto_ptr`:

```
// Example 6: Never try to do work through
//            a non-owning auto_ptr
//
void f()
{
  auto_ptr<T> pt1( new T );
  auto_ptr<T> pt2;
  pt2 = pt1;  // now pt2 owns the pointer, and
              // pt1 does not
  pt1->DoSomething();
              // error: following a null pointer
}
```

With that in mind, we start to see how well `auto_ptr` works with sources and sinks. A "source" is a function or other operation that creates a new resource, and then it typically hands off and relinquishes ownership of the resource. A "sink" is a function that does the reverse—namely, that takes ownership of an existing object (and typically disposes of it). Instead of just having sources and sinks return and take bald pointers, though, it's usually better to return or take a smart pointer that owns the resource.

This gets us to the first part of the Item's code:

```
auto_ptr<T> source()
{
  return auto_ptr<T>( new T(1) );
}
void sink( auto_ptr<T> pt ) { }
```

This is both legal and safe. Note the elegance of what's going on here:

1. `source()` allocates a new object and returns it to the caller in a completely safe way, by letting the caller assume ownership of the pointer. Even if the caller ignores the return value (of course, you would never write code that ignores return values, right?), the allocated object will always be safely deleted.

   See also Item 19, which demonstrates why this is an important idiom, since returning a result by wrapping it in something like an `auto_ptr` is sometimes the only way to make a function strongly exception-safe.
2. `sink()` takes an `auto_ptr` by value and therefore assumes ownership of it. When `sink()` is done, the deletion is performed as the local `auto_ptr` object goes out of scope (as long as `sink()` itself hasn't handed off ownership to someone else). Because the `sink()` function as written above doesn't actually do anything with the parameter, calling "`sink( pt );`" is a fancy way of writing "`pt.reset(0);`".

The next piece of code shows `source()` and `sink()` in action.

```
void f()
{
  auto_ptr<T> a( source() );
```

This is again both legal and safe. Here `f()` takes ownership of the pointer received from `source()`, and (ignoring some problems later in `f()`) it will delete it automatically when the automatic variable goes out of scope. This is fine, and it's exactly how passing back an `auto_ptr` by value is meant to work.

```
  sink( source() );
```

Once again, this is both legal and safe. Given the trivial (that is, empty) definitions of `source()` and `sink()` here, this is just a fancy way of writing "`delete new T(1);`". So is it really useful? Well, if you imagine `source()` as a nontrivial factory function and `sink()` as a nontrivial consumer, then yes, it makes a lot of sense and crops up regularly in real-world programming.

```
  sink( auto_ptr<T>( new T(1) ) );
```

Still legal and safe. This is another fancy way of writing "`delete new T(1);`", and it's a useful idiom when `sink()` is a nontrivial consumer function that takes ownership of the pointed-to object.

But beware: Never use `auto_ptr`s except in one of the ways I've just described. I have seen many programmers try to use `auto_ptr`s in other ways, just as they would use any other object. The problem with this is that `auto_ptr`s are most assuredly *not* like any other object. Here's the fundamental issue, and I'll highlight it to make sure it stands out.

For `auto_ptr`, copies are NOT equivalent.

It turns out that this has important effects when you try to use `auto_ptr`s with generic code that does make copies and isn't necessarily aware that copies aren't equivalent (after all, copies usually are). Consider the following code that I regularly see posted on the C++ newsgroups:

```
  vector< auto_ptr<T> > v;
```

This is not legal, and it sure isn't safe! Beware—this road is paved with good intentions.

It is *never* safe to put `auto_ptr`s into standard containers. Some people will tell you that their compiler and library compiles this fine, and others will tell you that they've seen exactly this example recommended in the documentation of a certain popular compiler. Don't listen to them.

The problem is that `auto_ptr` does not quite meet the requirements of a type you can put into containers, because copies of `auto_ptr`s are not equivalent. For one thing, there's nothing that says a `vector` can't just decide to up and make an "extra" internal copy of some object it contains. But hold on, because it's about to get worse.

```
  v.push_back( auto_ptr<T>( new T(3) ) );
  v.push_back( auto_ptr<T>( new T(4) ) );
  v.push_back( auto_ptr<T>( new T(1) ) );
  v.push_back( a );
```

(Note that copying a into v means that the a object no longer owns the pointer it's carrying. More on that in a moment.)

```
v.push_back( auto_ptr<T>( new T(2) ) );
sort( v.begin(), v.end() );
```

Illegal. Unsafe. When you call generic functions that will copy elements, like sort() does, the functions have to be able to assume that copies are going to be equivalent. At least one popular sort internally takes a copy of a "pivot" element, and if you try to make it work on auto_ptrs, it will merrily take a copy of the pivot auto_ptr object (thereby taking ownership and putting it in a temporary auto_ptr on the side), do the rest of its work on the sequence (including taking further copies of the now-nonowning auto_ptr that was picked as a pivot value), and when the sort is over, the pivot is destroyed and you have a problem. At least one auto_ptr in the sequence no longer owns the pointer it once held, and in fact the pointer it held has already been deleted.

So the standards committee bent over backward to do everything it could to help you out. The standard auto_ptr was deliberately and specifically designed to break if you try to use it with the standard containers (or, at least, to break with most natural implementations of the standard library). To do this, the committee used a trick: auto_ptr's copy constructor and copy assignment operator take references to non-const to the right-hand-side object. Most implementations of the standard containers' single-element insert() functions take a reference to const, and hence won't work with auto_ptrs.

The Scoop on Nonowning auto_ptrs

```
    // (after having copied a to another auto_ptr)
  cout << a->Value();
}
```

(We'll assume that a was copied, but that its pointer wasn't deleted by the vector or the sort.) Copying an auto_ptr not only transfers ownership, but resets the source auto_ptr to null. This is done specifically to avoid letting anyone do anything through a nonowning auto_ptr. Using a nonowning auto_ptr like this is not legal, and trying to dereference a null pointer like this will result in undefined behavior (typically, a core dump or memory access exception on most systems).

This brings us to the last common usage of auto_ptr.

Wrapping Pointer Members

```
class C
{
public:    /*...*/
protected: /*...*/
private:   /*...*/
  auto_ptr<CImpl> pimpl_;
};
```

Possible issue: One of the /*...*/ areas (whether public, protected, or private) had better include at least declarations for copy construction and copy assignment.

auto_ptrs are useful for encapsulating pointing member variables. This works very much like our motivating example at the beginning of this Item, except that instead of saving us the trouble of doing cleanup at the end of a function, it now saves us the trouble of doing cleanup in C's destructor.

There is still a caveat, of course: Just as if you were using a bald pointer data member instead of an auto_ptr member, you will have to supply your own destructor and copy constructor and copy assignment operator for the class (even if you disable them by making them private and undefined), because the default ones will do the wrong thing.

auto_ptr and Exception Safety

Finally, auto_ptr is sometimes essential to writing exception-safe code. Consider the following function:

```
// Exception-safe?
//
String f()
{
    String result;
    result = "some value";
    cout << "some output";
    return result;
}
```

This function has two visible side effects: It emits some output, and it returns a String. A detailed examination of exception safety is beyond the scope of this Item, but the goal we want to achieve is the strong exception-safety guarantee, which boils down to ensuring that the function acts atomically—even if there are exceptions, either all side effects will happen or none of them will.

Although the above code comes pretty close to achieving the strong exception-safety guarantee, there's still one minor quibble, as illustrated by the following calling code:

```
String theName;
theName = f();
```

The String copy constructor is invoked because the result is returned by value, and the copy assignment operator is invoked to copy the result into theName. If either copy fails, then f() has completed all of its work and all of its side effects (good), but the result has been irretrievably lost (oops).

Can we do better, and perhaps avoid the problem by avoiding the copy? For example, we could let the function take a non-const String reference parameter and place the return value in that:

```
// Better?
//
void f( String& result )
```

```
{
  cout << "some output";
  result = "some value";
}
```

This may look better, but it isn't, because the assignment to result might still fail which leaves us with one side effect complete and the other incomplete. Bottom line, this attempt doesn't really buy us much.

One way to solve the problem is to return a pointer to a dynamically allocated `String`, but the best solution is to go a step farther and return the pointer in an `auto_ptr`:

```
// Correct (finally!)
//
auto_ptr<String> f()
{
  auto_ptr<String> result = new String;
  *result = "some value";
  cout << "some output";
  return result;
      // rely on transfer of
      // ownership; this can't throw
}
```

This does the trick, since we have effectively hidden all of the work to construct the second side effect (the return value) while ensuring that it can be safely returned to the caller using only nonthrowing operations after the first side effect has completed (the printing of the message). We know that, once the `cout` is complete, the returned value will make it successfully into the hands of the caller, and be correctly cleaned up in all cases: If the caller accepts the returned value, the act of accepting a copy of the `auto_ptr` causes the caller to take ownership; and if the caller does not accept the returned value, say by ignoring the return value, the allocated `String` will be automatically cleaned up as the temporary `auto_ptr` holding it is destroyed. The price for this extra safety? As often happens when implementing strong exception safety, the strong safety comes at the (usually minor) cost of some efficiency—here, the extra dynamic memory allocation. But, when it comes to trading off efficiency for correctness, we usually ought to prefer the latter!

Make a habit of using smart pointers like `auto_ptr` in your daily work. `auto_ptr` neatly solves common problems and will make your code safer and more robust, especially when it comes to preventing resource leaks and ensuring strong exception safety. Because it's standard, it's portable across libraries and platforms, and so it will be right there with you wherever you take your code.

The `const auto_ptr` Idiom

Now that we've waded through the deeper stuff, here's a technique you'll find interesting. Among its other benefits, the refinement to `auto_ptr` also means that `const auto_ptrs` never lose ownership. Copying a `const auto_ptr` is illegal, and in fact the only things you can do with a `const auto_ptr` are dereference it with `operator*()` or `operator->()` or call get() to inquire about the value of the contained pointer. This means that we have a clear and concise idiom to express that an auto_ptr can never lose ownership.

```
const auto_ptr<T> pt1( new T );
    // making pt1 const guarantees that pt1 can
    // never be copied to another auto_ptr, and
    // so is guaranteed to never lose ownership
auto_ptr<T> pt2( pt1 ); // illegal
auto_ptr<T> pt3;
pt3 = pt1;              // illegal
pt1.release();          // illegal
pt1.reset( new T );     // illegal
```

Now that's what I call const. So if you want to declare to the world that an auto_ptr can never be changed and will always delete what it owns, this is the way to do it. The const auto_ptr idiom is a useful and common technique, and one you should keep in mind. The originally posted solution to this *Guru of the Week* issue concluded with the following words: "This const auto_ptr idiom is one of those things that's likely to become a commonly used technique, and now you can say that you knew about it since the beginning."

Traps, Pitfalls, and Anti-Idioms

Item 38: Object Identity — Difficulty: 5

"Who am I, really?" This problem addresses how to decide whether two pointers really refer to the same object.

The "`this != &other`" test (illustrated below) is a common coding practice intended to prevent self-assignment. Is the condition necessary and/or sufficient to accomplish this? Why or why not? If not, how would you fix it?

```
T& T::operator=( const T& other )
{
  if( this != &other )    // the test in question
  {
    // ...
  }
  return *this;
}
```

Remember to distinguish between "protecting against Murphy versus protecting against Machiavelli"—that is, protecting against things going wrong on their own versus a malicious programmer going to great lengths trying to break your code.

Solution

Short answer: In most cases, it's bad only if, without the test, self-assignment is not handled correctly. Although this check won't protect against all possible abuses, in practice it's fine as long as it's being done for optimization only. In the past, some have suggested that multiple inheritance affects the correctness of this problem. This is not true, and it's a red herring.

Exception Safety (Murphy)

If `T::operator=()` is written using the create-a-temporary-and-swap idiom (see page 47), it will be both strongly exception-safe and not *have* to test for self-assignment. Period. Because we should normally prefer to write copy assignment this way, we shouldn't need to perform the self-assignment test, right?

> **Guideline**
>
> *Never write a copy assignment operator that relies on a check for self-assignment in order to work properly; a copy assignment operator that uses the create-a-temporary-and-swap idiom is automaticially both strongly exception-safe and safe for self-assignment,*

Yes and no. It turns out that there are two potential efficiency costs when not checking for self-assignment.

- If you can test for self-assignment, then you can completely optimize away the assignment
- Often making code exception-safe also makes it less efficient (a.k.a. the "paranoia has a price principle").

In practice, if self-assignment happens often (rare, in most programs) and the speed improvement gained by suppressing unnecessary work during self-assignment is significant to your application (even rarer, in most programs), check for self-assignment.

> **Guideline**
>
> *It's all right to use a self-assignment check as an optimization to avoid needless work.*

Operator Overloading (Machiavelli?)

Because classes may provide their own `operator&()`, the test in question may do something completely different than is intended. This comes under the heading of "protecting against Machiavelli," though; presumably, the writer of `T::operator=()` knows whether his class also overloads `T::operator&()`. Of course, a base class could also provide `operator&()` in a way that breaks this test.

Note that while a class may also provide a `T::operator!=()`, this is irrelevant because it can't interfere with the "`this != &other`" test. The reason is that you can't write an `operator!=()` that takes two `T*` parameters, because at least one parameter of an overloaded operator must be of class type.

Postscript #1:

As a bonus, here's a little code joke. Believe it or not, it's been tried by well-meaning (although clearly misguided) coders.

```
T::T( const T& other )
{
  if( this != &other )
  {
    // ...
  }
}
```

Did you get the point on first reading?[1]

Postscript #2

Note that there are other cases in which pointer comparison is not what most people would consider intuitive. Here are a couple of examples.

- Comparing pointers into string literals is undefined. The reason is that the standard explicitly allows compilers to store string literals in overlapping areas of memory as a space optimization. For this reason, it's entirely possible to take a pointer into two different string literals and have them compare equal.
- In general, you cannot compare arbitrary bald pointers using the builtin operators <, <=, >, and >= with well-defined results, although the results are defined in specific situations (for example, pointers to objects in the same array can be so compared). The standard library works around this limitation by saying that the library's comparison function templates, `less<>` and its brothers, must give an ordering of pointers. This is necessary so that you can create, say, a `map` with keys of pointer type—for example, a `map<T*,U>` that, with the default template parameter, is a `map<T*,U,less<T*> >`.

---

1. Checking for self-assignment in a constructor doesn't make sense, because the `other` object can't be the same as our own object—our own object is still in the process of being created! When I first wrote that code joke, I thought (correctly) that the test should be meaningless. Still, it turns out that this one actually falls into the category of "protecting against Machiavelli." Friend and astute reader Jim Hyslop pointed out that there is a piece of (technically illegal) code using placement `new` that, if it were legal, would make the test meaningful:

```
T t;
new (&t) T(t);  // illegal, but it would make the test meaningful
```

Yikes! I'm not sure whether to be happy that people appreciated my code joke, or to be deeply worried that they immediately started trying to find subversive ways to make it meaningful.

Similarly, the following code is also not valid C++, in that it's syntactically legal (a conforming compiler must accept it) but has undefined behavior (a conforming compiler may legitimately emit code that will reformat your hard drive). If the code were valid, it would also make the test meaningful:

```
T t = t; // invalid, but it would make the test meaningful
```

Item 39: Automatic Conversions — Difficulty: 4

Automatic conversions from one type to another can be extremely convenient. This Item covers a typical example to illustrate why they're also extremely dangerous.

The standard C++ `string` has no implicit conversion to a `const char*`. Should it?

It is often useful to be able to access a `string` as a C-style `const char*`. Indeed, `string` has a member function `c_str()` to allow just that, by giving access to a `const char*`. Here's the difference in client code:

```
string s1("hello"), s2("world");
strcmp( s1, s2 );                  // 1 (error)
strcmp( s1.c_str(), s2.c_str() ) // 2 (ok)
```

It would certainly be nice to do #1, but #1 is an error because `strcmp` requires two pointers and there's no automatic conversion from `string` to `const char*`. Number 2 is okay, but it's longer to write because we have to call `c_str()` explicitly.

So this Item's question really boils down to: Wouldn't it be better if we could just write #1?

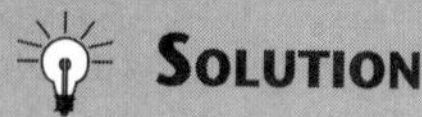

Solution

The question was: The standard C++ `string` has no implicit conversion to a `const char*`. Should it?

The answer is: No, with good reason.

It's almost always a good idea to avoid writing automatic conversions, either as conversion operators or as single-argument non-`explicit` constructors.[2] The main reasons that implicit conversions are unsafe in general are:

- Implicit conversions can interfere with overload resolution.
- Implicit conversions can silently let "wrong" code compile cleanly.

If a `string` had an automatic conversion to `const char*`, that conversion could be implicitly called anywhere the compiler felt it was necessary. What this means is that you would get all sorts of subtle conversion problems—the same ones you get into when you have non-`explicit` conversion constructors. It becomes far too easy to write code that looks right, is in fact not right and should fail, but by sheer coincidence will compile by doing something completely different from what was intended.

---

2. This solution focuses on the usual problems of implicit conversions, but there are other reasons why a `string` class should not have a conversion to `const char*`. Here are a few citations to further discussions: Koenig A. and Moo B. *Ruminations on C++* (Addison Wesley Longman, 1997), pages 290–292. Stroustrup, Bjarne. *The Design and Evolution of C++* (Addison-Wesley, 1994), page 83.

There are many good examples. Here's a simple one:

```
string s1, s2, s3;
s1 = s2 - s3;    // oops, probably meant "+"
```

The subtraction is meaningless and should be wrong. If `string` had an implicit conversion to `const char*`, however, this code would compile cleanly because the compiler would silently convert both strings to `const char*`'s and then subtract those pointers.

Guideline

Avoid writing conversion operators. Avoid non-`explicit` constructors.

Item 40: Object Lifetimes—Part 1 Difficulty: 5

"To be, or not to be..." When does an object actually exist? This problem considers when an object is safe to use.

Critique the following code fragment.

```
void f()
{
  T t(1);
  T& rt = t;
  //--- #1: do something with t or rt ---
  t.~T();
  new (&t) T(2);
  //--- #2: do something with t or rt ---
} // t is destroyed again
```

Is the code in block #2 safe and/or legal? Explain.

Solution

Yes, #2 is safe and legal (if you get to it), but:

- The function as a whole is not safe.
- It's a bad habit to get into.

The C++ standard explicitly allows this code. The reference `rt` is not invalidated by the in-place destruction and reconstruction. (Of course, you can't use `t` or `rt` between the call to `t.~T()` and the placement `new`, because during that time no object exists. We're also forced to assume that `T::operator&()` hasn't been overloaded to do something other than return the object's address.)

The reason we say #2 is safe "if you get to it" is that `f()` as a whole may not be exception-safe.

The function is not safe. If `T`'s constructor may throw in the `new (&t) T(2)` call, then `f()` is not exception-safe. Consider why: If the `T(2)` call throws, then no new object has been reconstructed in the `t` memory area, yet at the end of the function, `T::~T()` is naturally called (since `t` is an automatic variable) and "t is destroyed again," just as the comment says. That is, `t` will be constructed once but destroyed twice (oops). This is likely to create unpredictable side effects, such as core dumps.

> **Guideline**
>
> *Always endeavor to write exception-safe code. Always structure code so that resources are correctly freed and data is in a consistent state even in the presence of exceptions.*

This is a bad habit. Ignoring the exception-safety issues, the code happens to work in this setting because the programmer knows the complete type of the object being constructed and destroyed. That is, the object was a `T` and is being destroyed and reconstructed as a `T`.

This technique is rarely, if ever, necessary in real code and is a very bad habit to get into, because it's fraught with (sometimes subtle) dangers if it appears in a member function.

```
// Can you spot the subtle problem?
//
void T::DestroyAndReconstruct( int i )
{
  this->~T();
  new (this) T(i);
}
```

Now is this technique safe? In general, no. Consider the following code.

```
class U : public T { /* ... */ };
void f()
{
  /*AAA*/ t(1);
  /*BBB*/& rt = t;
  //--- #1: do something with t or rt ---
  t.DestroyAndReconstruct(2);
  //--- #2: do something with t or rt ---
} // t is destroyed again
```

If "`/*AAA*/`" is "`T`", the code in #2 will still work, even if "`/*BBB*/`" is not "`T`" (it could be a base class of `T`).

If "`/*AAA*/`" is "`U`", all bets are off, no matter what "`/*BBB*/`" is. Probably, the best you can hope for is an immediate core dump, because the call `t.DestroyAndReconstruct()` "slices" the object. Here, the slicing issue is that `t.DestroyAndReconstruct()` replaces the original object with another object of a different type—that is, a `T` instead of a `U`. Even if you're willing to write nonportable code, there's no way of knowing whether the object layout of a `T` is even usable as a `U` when it's superimposed in memory where a `U` used to be. Chances are good that it's not.

Don't go there. This is never a good practice.

Guideline

Avoid the "dusty corners" of a language; use the simplest techniques that are effective.

This Item has covered some basic safety and slicing issues of in-place destruction and reconstruction. This sets the stage for the followup question in Item 41.

Item 41: Object Lifetimes—Part 2 Difficulty: 6

Following from Item 40, this issue considers a C++ idiom that's frequently recommended—but often dangerously wrong.

Critique the following "anti-idiom" (shown as commonly presented).

```
T& T::operator=( const T& other )
{
  if( this != &other )
  {
    this->~T();
    new (this) T(other);
  }
  return *this;
}
```

1. What legitimate goal does it try to achieve? Correct any coding flaws in this version.
2. Even with any flaws corrected, is this idiom safe? Explain. If not, how else should the programmer achieve the intended results?

   (See also Item 40.)

Solution

This idiom[3] is frequently recommended, and it appears as an example in the C++ standard (see the discussion in the accompanying box). It is also exceedingly poor form and causes no end of problems. Don't do it.

Fortunately, as we'll see, there is a right way to get the intended effect.

3. I'm ignoring pathological cases (for example, overloading `T::operator&()` to do something other than `return this`). See also Item 38.

A Warning Example

In the C++ standard, this example was intended to demonstrate the object lifetime rules, not to recommend a good practice (it isn't). For those interested, here it is, slightly edited for space, from clause 3.8, paragraph 7:

```
[Example:
  struct C {
    int i;
    void f();
    const C& operator=( const C& );
  };
  const C& C::operator=( const C& other)
  {
    if ( this != &other )
    {
      this->~C();      // lifetime of *this ends
      new (this) C(other);
                       // new object of type C created
      f();             // well-defined
    }
    return *this;
  }
  C c1;
  C c2;
  c1 = c2; // well-defined
  c1.f();  // well-defined; c1 refers to a new object of type C
--end example]
```

As further proof that this is not intended to recommend good practice, note that here `C::operator=()` returns a `const C&` rather than a plain `C&`, which needlessly prevents portable use of these objects in standard library containers.

From the PeerDirect coding standards:

- declare copy assignment as `T& T::operator=(const T&)`
- don't return `const T&`. Though this would be nice, because it prevents usage such as "`(a=b)=c`", it would mean that, for example, you couldn't portably put `T` objects into standard library containers, since these require that assignment returns a plain `T&` (see also Cline95: 212; Murray93: 32-33)

Now let's look at the questions again.

1. What legitimate goal does it try to achieve?

This idiom expresses copy assignment in terms of copy construction. That is, it's trying to make sure that `T`'s copy assignment and its copy constructor do the same thing, which keeps the programmer from having to needlessly repeat the same code in two places.

This is a noble goal. After all, it makes programming easier when you don't have to write the same thing twice, and if `T` changes (for example, gets a new member variable) you can't forget to update one of the functions when you update the other.

This idiom could be particularly useful when there are virtual base classes that have data members, which would otherwise be assigned incorrectly at worst or multiple times at best. While this sounds good, it's not really much of a benefit in reality, because virtual base classes shouldn't have data members anyway (see Meyers98, Meyers99, and Barton94). Also, if there are virtual base classes, it means that this class is designed for inheritance, which (as we're about to see) means we can't use this idiom—it is too dangerous.

The rest of the first question was: Correct any coding flaws in the version above.

The above code has one flaw that can be corrected, and several others that cannot.

Problem 1: It Can Slice Objects

The code "`this->~T(); new (this) T(other);`" does the wrong thing if `T` is a base class with a virtual destructor. When called on an object of a derived class, it will destroy the derived object and replace it with a `T` object. This will almost certainly break any subsequent code that tries to use the object. See Item 40 for further discussion of slicing.

In particular, this makes life a royal pain for authors of derived classes (and there are other potential traps for derived classes; see below). Recall that derived assignment operators are usually written in terms of the base's assignment, as follows:

```
Derived&
Derived::operator=( const Derived& other )
{
  Base::operator=( other );
  // ...now assign Derived members here...
  return *this;
}
```

In this case, we get:

```
class U : T { /* ... */ };
U& U::operator=( const U& other )
{
  T::operator=( other );
  // ...now assign U members here...
  //    ...oops, but we're not a U any more!
  return *this;  // likewise oops
}
```

As written, the call to `T::operator=()` silently breaks all the code after it (both the `U` member assignments and the return statement). This often manifests as a mysterious and hard-to-debug run-time error if the `U` destructor doesn't reset its data members to invalid values.

To correct this problem, we could try a couple of alternatives.

- Should `U`'s copy assignment operator call "`this->T::~T();`" instead, perhaps followed by a placement `new` of the `T` base subobject? Well, that would ensure that for a derived object, only the `T` base subobject will be replaced (rather than have the whole derived object sliced and wrongly transformed into a `T`). It turns out that there are pitfalls with this approach, but let's keep this idea active for now.
- So should we go a step further, and have `U`'s copy assignment operator follow `T`'s idiom of in-place destruction (of the whole `U` object) and placement reconstruction? This is a

better alternative than the previous one, but it well illustrates a secondary weakness of the idiom. If one class uses this idiom, then all its derived classes must use the idiom, too. (This is a bad thing for many reasons, not the least of which is that the default compiler-generated copy assignment operator doesn't use this idiom, and many programmers who derive without adding data members won't even think of providing their own version of `operator=()`, thinking that the compiler-generated one ought to be okay.)

Alas, both of these patchwork solutions only replace an obvious danger with a subtler one that can still affect authors of derived classes (see below).

Guideline

Avoid the "dusty corners" of a language; use the simplest techniques that are effective.

Guideline

Avoid unnecessarily terse or clever code, even if it's perfectly clear to you when you first write it.

Now for the second question: Even with any flaws corrected, is this idiom safe? Explain.

No. Note that none of the following problems can be fixed without giving up on the entire idiom.

Problem 2: It's Not Exception-Safe

The `new` statement will invoke the `T` copy constructor. If that constructor can throw (and many classes do report constructor errors by throwing an exception), then the function is not exception-safe, because it will end up destroying the old object without replacing it with anything.

Like slicing, this flaw will break any subsequent code that tries to use the object. Worse, it will probably cause the program to attempt to destroy the same object twice, because the outside code has no way of knowing that the destructor for this object has already been run. (See Item 40 for further discussion of double destruction.)

Guideline

Always endeavor to write exception-safe code. Always structure code so that resources are correctly freed and data is in a consistent state even in the presence of exceptions.

Problem 3: It Changes Normal Object Lifetimes

This idiom breaks any code that relies on normal object lifetimes. In particular, it breaks or interferes with all classes that use the common "resource acquisition is initialization" idiom. In general, it breaks or interferes with any class whose constructor or destructor has side effects.

For example, what if `T` (or any base class of `T`) acquires a mutex lock or starts a database transaction in its constructor and frees the lock or transaction in its destructor? Then the lock/transaction will be incorrectly released and reacquired during an assignment—typically breaking both client code and the class itself. Besides `T` and `T`'s base classes, this can also break `T`'s derived classes if they rely on `T`'s normal lifetime semantics.

Some will say, "But I'd never do this in a class that acquires/releases a mutex in its constructor/destructor!" The short answer is, "Really? And how do you know that none of your (direct or indirect) base classes does so?" Frankly, you often have no way of knowing this, and you should never rely on your base classes working properly in the face of playing unusual games with object lifetimes.

The fundamental problem is that this idiom subverts the meaning of construction and destruction. Construction and destruction correspond exactly to the beginning/end of an object's lifetime, at which times the object typically acquires/releases resources. Construction and destruction are not meant to be used to change an object's value (and in fact they do not; they actually destroy the old object and replace it with a lookalike that happens to carry the new value, which is not the same thing at all).

Problem 4: It Can Still Break Derived Classes

With Problem 1 solved using the first approach, namely calling "`this->T::~T();`" instead, this idiom replaces only the "`T` part" (or `T` base subobject) within a derived object. For one thing, this should make us nervous because it subverts C++'s usual guarantee that base subobject lifetimes embrace the complete derived object's lifetime—that base subobjects are always constructed before, and destroyed after, the complete derived object. In practice, many derived classes may react well to having their objects' base parts swapped out and in like this, but some may not.

In particular, any derived class that takes responsibility for its base class's state could fail if its base parts are modified without its knowledge (and invisibly destroying and reconstructing an object certainly counts as modification). This danger can be mitigated as long as the assignment doesn't do anything more extraordinary or unexpected than a "normally written" assignment operator would do.

Problem 5: `this != &other`

The idiom relies completely on the `this != &other` test. (If you doubt that, consider what happens in the case of self-assignment if the test isn't performed.)

The problem is the same as the one we covered in Item 38: Any copy assignment that is written in such a way that it *must* check for self-assignment is probably not strongly exception-safe.[4]

4. There's nothing wrong with using the `this != &other` test to optimize away known self-assignments. If it works, you've saved yourself an assignment. If it doesn't, of course, your assignment operator should still be written in such a way that it's safe for self-assignment. There are arguments both for and against using this test as an optimization, but that's beyond the scope of this Item.

This idiom harbors other potential hazards that can affect client code and/or derived classes (such as behavior in the presence of virtual assignment operators, which are always a bit tricky at the best of times), but this should be enough to demonstrate that the idiom has some serious problems.

And for the last part of the second question: If not, how else should the programmer achieve the intended results?

Expressing copy assignment in terms of copy construction is a good idea, but the right way to do it is to use the canonical (not to mention elegant) form of strongly exception-safe copy assignment. Provide a `Swap()` member that is guaranteed not to throw and that simply swaps the guts of this object with another one as an atomic operation, then write the copy assignment operator as follows:

```
T& T::operator=( const T& other )
{
  T temp( other );  // do all the work off to the side
  Swap( temp );     // then "commit" the work using only
  return *this;     //    nonthrowing operations
}
```

This method still implements copy assignment in terms of copy construction, but it does it the right, safe, low-calorie, and wholesome way. It doesn't slice objects; it's strongly exception-safe; it doesn't play games with normal object lifetimes; and it doesn't rely on checks for self-assignment.

For more about this canonical form and the different levels of exception-safety, see also Items 8 through 17, and 40.

So, in conclusion, the original idiom is full of pitfalls; it's often wrong; and it makes life a royal pain for the authors of derived classes. I'm sometimes tempted to post the problem code in the office kitchen with the caption: "Here be dragons."[5]

Guideline

Prefer providing a nonthrowing `Swap()` *and implement copy assignment in terms of copy construction as follows:*

```
// GOOD
T& T::operator=( const T& other )
{
  T temp( other );
  Swap( temp );
  return *this;
}
```

5. True, none of the solutions presented here works for classes with reference members—but that's not a limitation of the solutions, it's a direct result of the fact that classes with reference members shouldn't be assigned. If one needs to change the object that a reference refers to, one really ought to be using a pointer instead.

Guideline

Never use the trick of implementing copy assignment in terms of copy construction by using an explicit destructor followed by placement `new`*, even though this trick crops up every three months on the newsgroups—that is, never write:*

```
// BAD
T& T::operator=( const T& other )
{
  if( this != &other)
  {
    this->~T();              // evil
    new (this) T( other );   // evil
  }
  return *this;
}
```

Some Advice in Favor of Simplicity

My best advice? Don't get fancy. Treat a new C++ feature just as you would treat a loaded automatic weapon in a crowded room. Never use it just because it looks nifty. Wait until you understand the consequences, don't get cute, write what you know, and know what you write.

Cuteness hurts, for at least two reasons. First, cute code hurts portability. The cute programming trick you used to good effect under one compiler may not work at all on another. Worse, the second compiler might accept the code, but produce unintended results. For a simple example, many compilers don't support default template arguments or template specialization, so any code that relies on those features is effectively nonportable today. For a subtler example, many compilers disagree on how to handle multiple active exceptions. And if you just did a double-take—thinking that multiple active exceptions aren't allowed (a popular misconception)—just imagine how the poor compiler manufacturers must lose sleep over it, since there can indeed be any number of simultaneously active exceptions during stack unwinding.

Second, cute code hurts maintainability. Always remember that someone will have to maintain what you write. What you consider a neat programming trick today will be cursed as an incomprehensible rat's nest tomorrow by the person maintaining your code—and that maintainer might be you. For example, a certain graphics library once made cute use of what was then a new language feature: operator overloading. Using this library, your client code to add a control widget to an existing window would look something like this:

```
Window  w( /*...*/ );
Control c( /*...*/ );
w + c;
```

Instead of being cute, the library writers should have followed Scott Meyers' excellent advice to "do as the `int`s do." That is, when using operator overloading or any other language feature for your own classes, when in doubt always make your class follow the same semantics as the builtin and standard library types.

Write what you know when writing code. Consciously try to restrict 90% of your coding to the language features you understand well enough to write correctly in your sleep (you do dream about C++ code, don't you?), and use the other 10% to gain experience with other features. For those newer to C++, this advice may at first mean using C++ as just a better C, and there's absolutely nothing wrong with that.

Next, know what you write. Be aware of the consequences of what your code actually does. Among other things, keep up your reading in books like this one; relevant Internet newsgroups, such as *comp.lang.c++.moderated* and *comp.std.c++*; and trade magazines, such as *C/C++ User's Journal*, and *Dr. Dobb's Journal*. You'll need that continuous self-improvement to stay current with and deepen your understanding of your chosen programming language.

To illustrate the importance of knowing what you write, consider the dangerous idiom that we just discussed in this Item—namely, the trick of trying to implement copy assignment in terms of explicit destruction followed by in-place `new`. This trick crops up regularly every few months on the C++ newsgroups, and those who promote it generally mean well, intending to avoid code duplication—but do these programmers really know what they write? Probably not, because there are subtle pitfalls here, some of them quite serious. This Item has covered most of them. There wasn't anything wrong with the original goal of improving consistency, but in this case, knowing what you write would lead the programmer to achieve consistency in a better way—for example, by having a common private member function that does the work and is called by both copy construction and copy assignment.

In short, avoid the dusty corners of the language, and remember that cuteness hurts in many ways. Above all, write what you know, and know what you write, and you're likely to do well.

Miscellaneous Topics

ITEM 42: VARIABLE INITIALIZATION—OR IS IT? DIFFICULTY: 3

This first problem highlights the importance of understanding what you write. Here we have four simple lines of code, no two of which mean the same thing, even though the syntax varies only slightly.

What is the difference, if any, between the following? (`T` stands for any class type.)

```
T t;
T t();
T t(u);
T t = u;
```

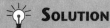

SOLUTION

This puzzle demonstrates the difference between three kinds of initialization: default initialization, direct initialization, and copy initialization. It also contains one red herring that isn't initialization at all. Let's consider the cases one by one.

```
T t;
```

This is *default initialization.* This code declares a variable named `t`, of type `T`, which is initialized using the default constructor `T::T()`.

```
T t();
```

A red herring. At first glance, it may look like just another variable declaration. In reality, it's a function declaration for a function named `t` that takes no parameters and returns a `T` object by value. (If you can't see this at first, consider that the above code is no different from writing something like `int f();` which is clearly a function declaration.)

Some people suggest writing "`auto T t();`" in an attempt to use the `auto` storage class to show that, yes, they really want a default-constructed variable named `t` of type `T`. Allow me license for a small rant here. For one thing, that won't work on a standard-conforming compiler; the compiler will still parse it as a function declaration, and then reject it because you can't specify an `auto` storage class for a return value. For another thing, even if it did work, it would be wrong-headed, because there's already a simpler way to do what's wanted. If you want a default-constructed variable `t` of type `T`, then just write "`T t;`" and quit trying to confuse the poor maintenance programmers with unnecessary subtlety. Always prefer simple solutions to cute solutions. Never write code that's any more subtle than necessary.

```
T t(u);
```

Assuming `u` is not the name of a type, this is *direct initialization*. The variable t is initialized directly from the value of `u` by calling `T::T(u)`. (If `u` is a type name, this is a declaration even if there is also a variable named `u` in scope; see above.)

```
T t = u;
```

This is *copy initialization*. The variable `t` is always initialized using `T`'s copy constructor, possibly after calling another function.

Common Mistake

This is always initialization; it is never assignment, and so it never calls `T::operator=()`. Yes, I know there's an "=" character in there, but don't let that throw you. That's just a syntax holdover from C, not an assignment operation.

Here are the semantics:

- If `u` is of type `T`, this is the same as writing "`T t(u);`" and just calls `T`'s copy constructor.
- If `u` is of some other type, then this has the meaning "`T t( T(u) );`"—that is, `u` is first converted to a temporary `T` object, and then `t` is copy-constructed from that. Note, however, that in this case the compiler is allowed to optimize away the "extra" copy and convert it to the direct-initialization form (that is, make it the same as "`T t(u);`"). If your compiler does this, the copy constructor must still be accessible. But if the copy constructor has side effects, then you may not get the results you expect, because the copy constructor's side effects may or may not happen, depending on whether the compiler performs the optimization or not.

Guideline

Prefer using the form "`T t(u);`" instead of "`T t = u;`" where possible. The former usually works wherever the latter works, and has other advantages—for example, it can take multiple parameters.

Item 43: Const-Correctness — Difficulty: 6

`const` is a powerful tool for writing safer code. Use `const` as much as possible, but no more. Here are some obvious and not-so-obvious places where `const` should—or shouldn't—be used.

Don't comment on or change the structure of this program; it's contrived and condensed for illustration only. Just add or remove `const` (including minor variants and related keywords) wherever appropriate.

Bonus question: In what places are the program's results undefined/uncompilable due to `const` errors?

```
class Polygon
{
public:
  Polygon() : area_(-1) {}
  void  AddPoint( const Point pt ) { InvalidateArea();
                                     points_.push_back(pt); }
  Point GetPoint( const int i )    { return points_[i]; }
  int   GetNumPoints()             { return points_.size(); }
  double GetArea()
  {
    if( area_ < 0 ) // if not yet calculated and cached
    {
      CalcArea();     // calculate now
    }
    return area_;
  }
private:
  void InvalidateArea() { area_ = -1; }
  void CalcArea()
  {
    area_ = 0;
    vector<Point>::iterator i;
    for( i = points_.begin(); i != points_.end(); ++i )
      area_ += /* some work */;
  }
  vector<Point> points_;
  double        area_;
};
Polygon operator+( Polygon& lhs, Polygon& rhs )
{
  Polygon ret = lhs;
  int last = rhs.GetNumPoints();
  for( int i = 0; i < last; ++i ) // concatenate
  {
    ret.AddPoint( rhs.GetPoint(i) );
  }
  return ret;
}
```

```
void f( const Polygon& poly )
{
  const_cast<Polygon&>(poly).AddPoint( Point(0,0) );
}

void g( Polygon& const rPoly ) { rPoly.AddPoint( Point(1,1) ); }

void h( Polygon* const pPoly ) { pPoly->AddPoint( Point(2,2) ); }

int main()
{
  Polygon poly;
  const Polygon cpoly;
  f(poly);
  f(cpoly);
  g(poly);
  h(&poly);
}
```

Solution

When I pose this kind of problem, I find that most people think the problem is on the easy side and address only the more-usual `const` issues. There are, however, subtleties that are worth knowing, hence this Item. See also the box "`const` and `mutable` Are Your Friends."

```
class Polygon
{
public:
  Polygon() : area_(-1) {}
  void  AddPoint( const  Point pt ) { InvalidateArea();
                                      points_.push_back(pt); }
```

1. The `Point` object is passed by value, so there is little or no benefit to declaring it `const`. In fact, to the compiler, the function signature is the same whether you include this `const` in front of a value parameter or not. For example:

```
int f( int );
int f( const int );  // redeclares f(int)
                     // no overloading, there's only one function
int g( int& );
int g( const int& ); // not the same as g(int&)
                     // g is overloaded
```

Guideline

Avoid `const` pass-by-value parameters in function declarations. Still make the parameter `const` in the same function's definition if it won't be modified.

```
Point GetPoint( const int i )    { return points_[i]; }
```

2. Same comment about the parameter type. Normally, `const` pass-by-value is unuseful and misleading at best.

3. This should be a `const` member function, since it doesn't change the state of the object.

4. If you're not returning a builtin type, such as `int` or `long`, return-by-value should usually return a `const` value.[1] This assists client code by making sure the compiler emits an error if the caller tries to modify the temporary.

For example, the user might write something like "`poly.GetPoint(i) = Point(2,2);`". If this were intended to work, `GetPoint()` should have used return-by-reference and not return-by-value in the first place. As we will see later, it makes sense for `GetPoint()` to be a `const` member function for another reason: `GetPoint()` should be usable on `const Polygon` objects in `operator+()`.

Guideline

When using return-by-value for non-builtin return types, prefer returning a `const` *value.*

```
int    GetNumPoints()               { return points_.size(); }
```

5. Again, the function should be `const`.

Incidentally, this is a good example of where not to write a `const` return-by-value. A return type of "`const int`" would be wrong in this case, because: (a) returning "`const int`" doesn't buy you anything, since the returned `int` is already an rvalue and so can't be modified; and (b) returning "`const int`" can interfere with template instantiation and is confusing, misleading, and probably fattening.

```
double GetArea()
{
  if( area_ < 0 ) // if not yet calculated and cached
  {
    CalcArea();      // calculate now
  }
  return area_;
}
```

6. Even though this function modifies the object's internal state, it should be `const`. Why? Because this function does not modify the object's observable state. We are doing some caching here, but that's an internal implementation detail and the object is logically `const` even if it isn't physically `const`.

1. I want to point out that not everyone agrees with me on this point. In Lakos96 (pg. 618), the author argues against returning a `const` value, and points out that it is redundant for builtin types anyway (for example, returning "`const int`"), which he notes may interfere with template instantiation.

Corollary: The member variable `area_` should be declared `mutable`. If your compiler doesn't support `mutable` yet, kludge this with a `const_cast` of `area_` and write a comment telling the next person to remove the `const_cast` once `mutable` is available—but do make the function `const`.

```
private:
  void InvalidateArea() { area_ = -1; }
```

7. This function ought also to be `const`, if for no other reason than consistency. Granted, semantically it will be called only from non-`const` functions, since its purpose is to invalidate the cached `area_` when the object's state changes. But consistency and clarity are important to good programming style, so make this function `const` too.

```
  void CalcArea()
  {
    area_ = 0;
    vector<Point>:: iterator  i;
    for( i = points_.begin(); i != points_.end(); ++i )
    {
      area_ += /* some work */;
    }
  }
```

8. This member function definitely should be `const`, because it does not alter the externally visible state of the object. Note also that this function is called only from another `const` member function, namely `GetArea()`.

9. The iterator should not change the state of the `points_` collection, so it ought to be a `const_iterator`.

```
  vector<Point> points_;
  double        area_;
};

Polygon operator+( Polygon&  lhs, Polygon&  rhs )
{
```

10. The parameters should be passed by references to `const`, of course.

11. Again, the return-by-value of an object should be `const`.

```
  Polygon ret = lhs;
  int  last = rhs.GetNumPoints();
```

12. Because `last` should never change, say so by making its type "`const int`".

```
  for( int i = 0; i < last; ++i ) // concatenate
  {
    ret.AddPoint( rhs.GetPoint(i) );
  }
  return ret;
}
```

(Once we make rhs a reference-to-const parameter, we see another reason why GetPoint() should be a const member function.)

```
void f( const Polygon& poly )
{
  const_cast<Polygon&>(poly).AddPoint( Point(0,0) );
}
```

Bonus: Using the result of the const_cast is undefined if the referenced object was declared as const—which it is in the case of f(cpoly) below. The parameter isn't really const, so don't declare it as const. It's tantamount to lying.

```
void g( Polygon& const rPoly ) { rPoly.AddPoint( Point(1,1) ); }
```

13. This const is not only useless, because references are already const inasmuch as they cannot be reseated (changed to refer to a different object), but actually illegal.

```
void h( Polygon* const pPoly ) { pPoly->AddPoint( Point(2,2) ); }
```

14. This const is equally useless, but for a different reason: Because we're passing the pointer by value, this makes as little sense as passing a parameter "const int" above. Think about it—it's exactly the same thing, because this const merely promises that you won't modify the pointer value. That's not a very useful promise, because the caller can't possibly care or be affected by that decision.

(If, in looking for the "bonus" part, you said something about this function being uncompilable—sorry, it's quite legal C++. You were probably thinking of putting the const to the left of the *, which would have made the function body illegal.)

```
int main()
{
  Polygon poly;
  const Polygon cpoly;
  f(poly);
```

This is fine.

```
  f(cpoly);
```

This causes undefined results when f() tries to cast away the const-ness of its parameter and then modify it. See above.

```
  g(poly);
```

This is fine.

```
  h(&poly);
}
```

This is fine.

const and mutable Are Your Friends

Be const-correct: const and mutable are your friends.

I still sometimes come across programmers who think const isn't worth the trouble. "Aw, const is a pain to write everywhere," I've heard some complain. "If I use it in one place, I have to use it all the time. And anyway, other people skip it, and their programs work fine. Some of the libraries I use aren't const-correct either. Is const worth it?"

We could imagine a similar scene, this time at a rifle range: "Aw, this gun's safety is a pain to set all the time. And anyway, some other people don't use it either, and some of them haven't shot their own feet off..."

Safety-incorrect riflemen are not long for this world. Nor are const-incorrect programmers, carpenters who don't have time for hard hats, and electricians who don't have time to identify the live wire. There is no excuse for ignoring the safety mechanisms provided with a product, and there is no excuse for programmers too lazy to write const-correct code. (Perhaps not strangely, the same people who skip const tend to ignore compiler warnings, too. Illuminating, that.) In many development shops, skipping const and ignoring compiler warnings are "one-warning" offences, and rightly so.

Using const whenever possible makes for safer, cleaner code. It lets you document interfaces and invariants far more effectively than any mere /* I promise not to change this */ comment can accomplish. It's a powerful part of "design by contract." It helps the compiler to stop you from accidentally writing bad code. It can even help the compiler to generate tighter, faster, smaller code. That being the case, there's no reason why you shouldn't use it as much as possible, and there's every reason why you should.

Remember that the correct use of mutable is a key part of const-correctness. If your class contains a member that could change even for const objects and operations, make that member mutable. That way, you will be able to write your class's const member functions easily and correctly, and users of your class will be able to correctly create and use const and non-const objects of your class's type.

It's true that not all commercial libraries' interfaces are const-correct. That isn't an excuse for you to write const-incorrect code, though. (It is, however, one of the few good excuses to write const_cast.) Always make your own code const-correct, and when you call the broken library, you can use the appropriate const_casts wherever necessary—preferably with a detailed comment nearby grumbling about the library vendor's laziness and how you're looking for a replacement product.

If you still harbor any doubts about const, run (don't walk) and reread Item 21, "Use const whenever possible," in Meyers98. It's for good reason that the C language has had const since the pre-standardization days. Back in the early 1980s, a researcher named Stroustrup had designed this funny little language called C with Classes, which had a funny little keyword called readonly that was demonstrably useful for specifying cleaner interfaces and, therefore, writing safer code. The C folks at Bell Labs liked the idea, but preferred the name const. When the ANSI C committee got rolling a short time later, they adopted the same feature with the same name—and the rest, as they say, is history (Stroustrup94, page 90).

Don't shoot yourself (or your fellow programmers) in the foot. Always check your safety: Be const-correct. Write const whenever possible, and smile at the thought of cleaner, safer, tighter code.

That's it. Here is a revised version of the code that corrects the `const` issues noted above (but does not attempt to correct any other poor style).

```
class Polygon
{
public:
  Polygon() : area_(-1) {}

  void        AddPoint( Point pt ) { InvalidateArea();
                                     points_.push_back(pt); }

  const Point GetPoint( int i ) const  { return points_[i]; }

  int         GetNumPoints() const { return points_.size(); }

  double GetArea() const
  {
    if( area_ < 0 ) // if not yet calculated and cached
      CalcArea();     // calculate now
    return area_;
  }

private:
  void InvalidateArea() const { area_ = -1; }

  void CalcArea() const
  {
    area_ = 0;
    vector<Point>::const_iterator i;
    for( i = points_.begin(); i != points_.end(); ++i )
      area_ += /* some work */;
  }

  vector<Point>  points_;
  mutable double area_;
};

const Polygon operator+( const Polygon& lhs,
                         const Polygon& rhs )
{
  Polygon ret = lhs;
  const int last = rhs.GetNumPoints();
  for( int i = 0; i < last; ++i ) // concatenate
    ret.AddPoint( rhs.GetPoint(i) );
  return ret;
}

void f( Polygon& poly )
{
  poly.AddPoint( Point(0,0) );
}

void g( Polygon& rPoly ) { rPoly.AddPoint( Point(1,1) ); }
void h( Polygon* pPoly ) { pPoly->AddPoint( Point(2,2) ); }
```

```
int main()
{
  Polygon poly;
  f(poly);
  g(poly);
  h(&poly);
}
```

Item 44: Casts — Difficulty: 6

How well do you know C++'s casts? Using them well can greatly improve the reliability of your code.

The new-style casts in standard C++ offer more power and safety than the old-style (C-style) casts. How well do you know them? The rest of this problem uses the following classes and global variables:

```
class  A { public: virtual ~A(); /*...*/ };
A::~A() { }

class B : private virtual A  { /*...*/ };

class C : public  A          { /*...*/ };

class D : public B, public C { /*...*/ };

A a1; B b1; C c1; D d1;
const A  a2;
const A& ra1 = a1;
const A& ra2 = a2;
char c;
```

This Item presents four questions.

1. Which of the following new-style casts are *not* equivalent to a C-style cast?

```
const_cast
dynamic_cast
reinterpret_cast
static_cast
```

2. For each of the following C-style casts, write the equivalent new-style cast. Which are incorrect if not written as a new-style cast?

```
void f()
{
  A* pa; B* pb; C* pc;
  pa = (A*)&ra1;
  pa = (A*)&a2;
  pb = (B*)&c1;
  pc = (C*)&d1;
}
```

3. Critique each of the following C++ casts for style and correctness.

```
void g()
{
  unsigned char* puc = static_cast<unsigned char*>(&c);
  signed char* psc = static_cast<signed char*>(&c);

  void* pv = static_cast<void*>(&b1);
  B* pb1 = static_cast<B*>(pv);

  B* pb2 = static_cast<B*>(&b1);

  A* pa1 = const_cast<A*>(&ra1);
  A* pa2 = const_cast<A*>(&ra2);

  B* pb3 = dynamic_cast<B*>(&c1);

  A* pa3 = dynamic_cast<A*>(&b1);

  B* pb4 = static_cast<B*>(&d1);

  D* pd = static_cast<D*>(pb4);

  pa1 = dynamic_cast<A*>(pb2);
  pa1 = dynamic_cast<A*>(pb4);

  C* pc1 = dynamic_cast<C*>(pb4);
  C& rc1 = dynamic_cast<C&>(*pb2);
}
```

4. Why is it typically unuseful to `const_cast` from non-`const` to `const`? Demonstrate a valid example in which it can be useful to `const_cast` from non-`const` to `const`.

Solution

Let's answer the questions one by one.

1. Which of the following new-style casts are *not* equivalent to a C-style cast?

Only `dynamic_cast` is not equivalent to a C-style cast. All other new-style casts have old-style equivalents.

Guideline

Prefer new-style casts.

2. For each of the following C-style casts, write the equivalent new-style cast. Which are incorrect if not written as a new-style cast?

```
void f()
{
  A* pa; B* pb; C* pc;
  pa = (A*)&ra1;
```

Use const_cast instead:

```
pa = const_cast<A*>(&ra1);
```

```
pa = (A*)&a2;
```

This cannot be expressed as a new-style cast. The closest candidate is const_cast, but because a2 is a const object, the results of using the pointer are undefined.

```
pb = (B*)&c1;
```

Use reinterpret_cast instead:

```
pb = reinterpret_cast<B*>(&c1);
```

```
  pc = (C*)&d1;
}
```

The above cast is wrong in C. In C++, no cast is required:

```
pc = &d1;
```

3. Critique each of the following C++ casts for style and correctness.

First, a general note: All of the following dynamic_casts would be errors if the classes involved did not have virtual functions. Fortunately, A does provide a virtual function, making all the dynamic_casts legal.

```
void g()
{
  unsigned char* puc = static_cast<unsigned char*>(&c);
  signed char* psc = static_cast<signed char*>(&c);
```

Error: We must use reinterpret_cast for both cases. This might surprise you at first, but the reason is that char, signed char, and unsigned char are three distinct types. Even though there are implicit conversions between them, they are unrelated, so pointers to them are unrelated.

```
void* pv = static_cast<void*> (&b1);
B* pb1 = static_cast<B*>(pv);
```

These are both fine, but the first is unnecessary, because there is already an implicit conversion from a data pointer to a void*.

```
B* pb2 = static_cast<B*> (&b1);
```

This is fine, but unnecessary, since the argument is already a B*.

```
A* pa1 = const_cast<A*>(&ra1);
```

This is legal, but casting away const (or volatile) is usually indicative of poor style. Most of the cases in which you legitimately would want to remove the const-ness of a pointer or reference are related to class members and covered by the `mutable` keyword. See Item 43 for further discussion of `const`-correctness.

Guideline

Avoid casting away `const`. *Use* `mutable` *instead.*

```
A* pa2 = const_cast<A*>(&ra2) ;
```

Error: This will produce undefined behavior if the pointer is used to write on the object, because `a2` really is a `const` object. To see why this is a legitimate problem, consider that a compiler is allowed to see that `a2` is created as a `const` object and use that information to store it in read-only memory as an optimization. Casting away `const` on such an object is obviously dangerous.

Guideline

Avoid casting away `const`.

```
B* pb3 = dynamic_cast<B*>(&c1) ;
```

Potential error (if you try to use `pb3`): Because `c1` IS-NOT-A `B` (because `C` is not publicly derived from `B`—in fact, it is not derived from `B` at all), this will set `pb3` to null. The only legal cast would be a `reinterpret_cast`, and using that is almost always evil.

```
A* pa3 = dynamic_cast<A*>(&b1) ;
```

Probable error: Because `b1` IS-NOT-AN `A` (because `B` is not publicly derived from `A`; its derivation is private), this is illegal unless `g()` is a friend of `B`.

```
B* pb4 = static_cast<B*>(&d1);
```

This is fine, but unnecessary because derived-to-public-base pointer conversions can be done implicitly.

```
D* pd = static_cast<D*>(pb4);
```

This is fine, which may surprise you if you expected this to require a `dynamic_cast`. The reason is that downcasts can be static when the target is known, but beware: You are telling the compiler that you know for a fact that what is being pointed to really is of that type. If you are wrong, then the cast cannot inform you of the problem (as could `dynamic_cast`, which would return a null pointer if the cast failed) and, at best, you will get spurious run-time errors and/or program crashes.

Guideline

Avoid downcasts.

```
        pa1 = dynamic_cast<A*>(pb2) ;
        pa1 = dynamic_cast<A*>(pb4);
```

These two look very similar. Both attempt to use `dynamic_cast` to convert a `B*` into an `A*`. However, the first is an error, while the second is not.

Here's the reason: As noted above, you cannot use `dynamic_cast` to cast a pointer to what really is a `B` object (and here `pb2` points to the object `b1`) into an `A` object, because `B` inherits privately, not publicly, from `A`. However, the second cast succeeds because `pb4` points to the object `d1`, and `D` does have `A` as an indirect public base class (through `C`), and `dynamic_cast` is able to cast across the inheritance hierarchy using the path `B*` → `D*` → `C*` → `A*`.

```
        C* pc1 = dynamic_cast<C*>(pb4);
```

This, too, is fine for the same reason as the last: `dynamic_cast` can navigate the inheritance hierarchy and perform cross-casts, so this is legal and will succeed.

```
        C& rc1 = dynamic_cast<C&>(*pb2) ;
    }
```

Finally, an "exceptional" error: Because `*pb2` isn't really a `C`, `dynamic_cast` will throw a `bad_cast` exception to signal failure. Why? Well, `dynamic_cast` can and does return null if a pointer cast fails, but since there's no such thing as a null reference, it can't return a null reference if a reference cast fails. There's no way to signal such a failure to the client code besides throwing an exception, so that's what the standard `bad_cast` exception class is for.

4. Why is it normally unuseful to `const_cast` from non-`const` to `const`?

The first three questions included no examples of using `const_cast` to add `const`, for example, to convert a pointer to non-`const` to a pointer to `const`. After all, explicitly adding `const` is usually redundant—for example, it's already legal to assign a pointer to non-`const` to a pointer to `const`. Normally, we only need `const_cast` to do the reverse.

And the last part of the question: Demonstrate a valid example where it can be useful to `const_cast` from non-`const` to `const`.

There is at least one case in which you could usefully `const_cast` from non-`const` to `const`—to call a specific overloaded function or a specific version of a template. For example:

```
void f( T& );
void f( const T& );
template<class T> void g( T& t )
{
  f( t );                          // calls f(T&)
  f( const_cast<const T&>(t) ); // calls f(const T&)
}
```

Of course, in the case of choosing a specific version of a template, it's usually just easier to name it explicitly instead of forcing the right deduction. For example, to call the right version of a templated function `h()`, writing "`h<const T&>( t )`" is preferable to writing "`h( const_cast<const T&>(t) )`".

Item 45: bool — Difficulty: 7

Do we really need a builtin `bool` type? Why not just emulate it in the existing language? This Item reveals the answer.

Besides `wchar_t` (which was a `typedef` in C), `bool` is the only builtin type to be added to C++ since the ARM (Ellis90).

Could `bool`'s effect have been duplicated without adding a builtin type? If yes, show an equivalent implementation. If no, show why possible implementations do not behave the same as the builtin `bool`.

Solution

The answer is: No, `bool`'s effect could not have been duplicated without adding a builtin type. The `bool` builtin type, and the reserved keywords `true` and `false`, were added to C++ precisely because they couldn't be duplicated completely using the existing language.

This Item is intended to illustrate the considerations you have to think about when you design your own classes, `enums`, and other tools.

The second part of the Item question was: If no, show why possible implementations do not behave the same as the builtin `bool`.

There are four major implementations.

Option 1: typedef (score: 8.5 / 10)

This option means to "`typedef <something> bool;`", typically:

```
// Option 1: typedef
//
typedef int bool;
const bool true  = 1;
const bool false = 0;
```

This solution isn't bad, but it doesn't allow overloading on `bool`. For example:

```
// file f.h
void f( int  ); // ok
void f( bool ); // ok, redeclares the same function
```

```
// file f.cpp
void f( int  ) { /*...*/ }    // ok
void f( bool ) { /*...*/ }    // error, redefinition
```

Another problem is that Option 1 can allow code like this to behave unexpectedly:

```
void f( bool b )
{
  assert( b != true && b != false );
}
```

So Option 1 isn't good enough.

Option 2: #define (score: 0 / 10)

This option means to "`#define bool` *<something>*", typically:

```
// Option 2: #define
//
#define bool  int
#define true  1
#define false 0
```

This is, of course, purely evil. It not only has all the same problems as Option 1, but it also wreaks the usual havoc of `#define`s. For example, pity the poor customer who tries to use this library and already has a variable named `false`; now this definitely behaves differently from a builtin type.

Trying to use the preprocessor to simulate a type is just a bad idea.

Option 3: enum (score: 9 / 10)

This option means to make an "`enum bool`", typically:

```
// Option 3: enum
//
enum bool { false, true };
```

This is somewhat better than Option 1. It allows overloading (the main problem with the first option), but it doesn't allow automatic conversions from a conditional expression (which would have been possible with the first option), to wit:

```
bool b;
b = ( i == j );
```

This doesn't work, because `int`s cannot be implicitly converted to `enum`s.

Option 4: Class (score: 9 / 10)

Hey, this is an object-oriented language, right? So why not write a class, typically:

```
class bool
{
public:
  bool();
  bool( int );            // to enable conversions from
  bool& operator=( int ); //  conditional expressions
  //operator int();   // questionable!
  //operator void*(); // questionable!
private:
  unsigned char b_;
};
const bool true ( 1 );
const bool false( 0 );
```

This works except for the conversion operators marked "questionable." They're questionable because:

- With an automatic conversion, `bool`s will interfere with overload resolution, just as do all classes having non-`explicit` (conversion) constructors and/or implicit conversion operators, especially when the conversion is from or to a common type. See Items 20 and 39 for more about implicit conversions.
- Without a conversion to something like `int` or `void*`, `bool` objects can't be tested "naturally" in conditions. For example:

  ```
  bool b;
  /*...*/
  if( b ) // error without an automatic conversion to
  {       // something like int or void*
      /*...*/
  }
  ```

It's a classic Catch-22 situation: We must choose one alternative or the other—either provide an automatic conversion or not—but neither option lets us duplicate the effect of having a builtin `bool` type. In summary:

- A `typedef ... bool` wouldn't allow overloading on bool.
- A `#define bool` wouldn't allow overloading either and would wreak the usual havoc of `#define`s.
- An `enum bool` would allow overloading but couldn't be automatically converted from a conditional expression (as in "`b = (i == j);`").
- A `class bool` would allow overloading but wouldn't let a `bool` object be tested in conditions (as in "`if( b )`") unless it provided an automatic conversion to something like `int` or `void*`, which would wreak the usual havoc of automatic conversions.

And, finally, there's one more thing (related to overloading) that we couldn't have done otherwise, either, except perhaps with the last option: Specify that conditional expressions have type `bool`.

So, yes, we really did need a builtin `bool`.

Item 46: Forwarding Functions — Difficulty: 3

What's the best way to write a forwarding function? The basic answer is easy, but we'll also learn about a subtle change to the language made shortly before the standard was finalized.

Forwarding functions are useful tools for handing off work to another function or object, especially when the hand-off is done efficiently.

Critique the following forwarding function. Would you change it? If so, how?

```
// file f.cpp
//
#include "f.h"
/*...*/
bool f( X x )
{
  return g( x );

}
```

Solution

Remember the introduction to the question? It was: Forwarding functions are useful tools for handing off work to another function or object, especially when the hand-off is done efficiently.

This introduction gets to the heart of the matter—efficiency.

There are two main enhancements that would make this function more efficient. The first should always be done; the second is a matter of judgment.

1. *Pass the parameter by* `const&` *instead of by value.*

"Isn't that blindingly obvious?" you might ask. No, it isn't, not in this particular case. Until as recently as 1997, the draft C++ language standard said that because a compiler can prove that the parameter `x` will never be used for any other purpose than passing it in turn to `g()`, the compiler may decide to elide `x` completely (that is, to eliminate `x` as unnecessary). For example, if the client code looks something like this:

```
X my_x;
f( my_x );
```

then the compiler used to be allowed to either:

- Create a copy of `my_x` for `f()`'s use (this is the parameter named `x` in `f()`'s scope) and pass that to `g()`
- Pass `my_x` directly to `g()` without creating a copy at all, because it notices that the extra copy will never be used except as a parameter to `g()`

The latter is nicely efficient, isn't it? That's what optimizing compilers are for, aren't they?

Yes and yes, until the London meeting in July 1997. At that meeting, the draft was amended to place more restrictions on the situations in which the compiler is allowed to elide "extra" copies like this. This change was necessary to avoid problems that can come up when compilers are permitted to wantonly elide copy construction, especially when copy construction has side effects. There are reasonable cases in which reasonable code may legitimately rely on the number of copies actually made of an object.

Today, the only situation in which a compiler may still elide copy constructors is for the return value optimization (see your favorite textbook for details) and for temporary objects. This means that for forwarding functions like `f()`, a compiler is now required to perform two copies. Because we (as the authors of `f()`) know in this case that the extra copy isn't necessary, we should fall back on our general rule and declare `x` as a `const X&` parameter.

Guideline

Prefer passing objects by reference instead of by value, using `const` *wherever possible.*

Note: If we'd been following this general rule all along instead of trying to take advantage of detailed knowledge about what the compiler is allowed to do, the change in the rules wouldn't have affected us. This is a stellar example of why simpler is better—avoid the dusty corners of the language as much as you can, and strive never to rely on cute subtleties.

Guideline

Avoid the "dusty corners" of a language; use the simplest techniques that are effective.

2. *Inline the function.* This one is a matter of judgment. In short, prefer to write all functions out-of-line by default, and then selectively inline individual functions as necessary only after you know that the performance gain from inlining is actually needed.

Guideline

Avoid inlining or detailed tuning until performance profiles prove the need.

If you inline the function, the positive side is that you avoid the overhead of the extra function call to f().

The negative side is that inlining f() exposes f()'s implementation and makes client code depend on it so that if f() changes, all client code must recompile. Worse, client code now also needs at least the prototype for function g(), which is a bit of a shame because client code never actually calls g() directly and probably never needed g()'s prototype before (at least, not as far as we can tell from our example). And if g() itself were changed to take other parameters of still other types, client code would now depend on those classes' declarations, too.

Both inlining and not inlining can be valid choices. It's a judgment call in which the benefits and drawbacks depend on what you know about how (and how widely) f() is used today, and how (and how often) it's likely to change in the future.

ITEM 47: CONTROL FLOW — DIFFICULTY: 6

How well do you really know the order in which C++ code is executed? Test your knowledge against this problem.

"The devil is in the details." Point out as many problems as possible in the following (somewhat contrived) code, focusing on those related to control flow.

```
#include <cassert>
#include <iostream>
#include <typeinfo>
#include <string>
using namespace std;

//  The following lines come from other header files.
//
char* itoa( int value, char* workArea, int radix );
extern int fileIdCounter;

//  Helpers to automate class invariant checking.
//
template<class T>
inline void AAssert( T& p )
{
  static int localFileId = ++fileIdCounter;
  if( !p.Invariant() )
  {
    cerr << "Invariant failed: file " << localFileId
         << ", " << typeid(p).name()
         << " at " << static_cast<void*>(&p) << endl;
    assert( false );
  }
}
```

```
template<class T>
class AInvariant
{
public:
  AInvariant( T& p ) : p_(p) { AAssert( p_ ); }
  ~AInvariant()              { AAssert( p_ ); }
private:
  T& p_;
};
#define AINVARIANT_GUARD AInvariant<AIType> invariantChecker( *this )

//--------------------------------------------------------------
template<class T>
class Array : private ArrayBase, public Container
{
  typedef Array AIType;
public:
  Array( size_t startingSize = 10 )
  : Container( startingSize ),
    ArrayBase( Container::GetType() ),
    used_(0),
    size_(startingSize),
    buffer_(new T[size_])
  {
    AINVARIANT_GUARD;
  }

  void Resize( size_t newSize )
  {
    AINVARIANT_GUARD;
    T* oldBuffer = buffer_;
    buffer_ = new T[newSize];
    copy( oldBuffer, oldBuffer+min(size_,newSize), buffer_ );
    delete[] oldBuffer;
    size_ = newSize;
  }

  string PrintSizes()
  {
    AINVARIANT_GUARD;
    char buf[30];
    return string("size = ") + itoa(size_,buf,10) +
           ", used = " + itoa(used_,buf,10);
  }

  bool Invariant()
  {
    if( used_ > 0.9*size_ ) Resize( 2*size_ );
    return used_ <= size_;
  }
private:
  T*     buffer_;
  size_t used_, size_;
};
```

```
int f( int& x, int y = x ) { return x += y; }
int g( int& x )            { return x /= 2; }

int main( int, char*[] )
{
  int i = 42;
  cout << "f(" << i << ") = " << f(i) << ", "
       << "g(" << i << ") = " << g(i) << endl;
  Array<char> a(20);
  cout << a.PrintSizes() << endl;
}
```

Solution

"Lions and tigers and bears, oh my!"—Dorothy

Compared with what's wrong with this Item's code, Dorothy had nothing to complain about. Let's consider it line by line.

```
#include <cassert>
#include <iostream>
#include <typeinfo>
#include <string>
using namespace std;

//  The following lines come from other header files.
//
char* itoa( int value, char* workArea, int radix );
extern int fileIdCounter;
```

The presence of a global variable should already put us on the lookout for clients that might try to use it before it has been initialized. The order of initialization for global variables (including class statics) between translation units is undefined.

> **Guideline**
>
> *Avoid using global or static objects. If you must use a global or static object, always be very careful about the order-of-initialization rules.*

```
//  Helpers to automate class invariant checking.
//
template<class T>
inline void AAssert( T& p )
{
  static int localFileId = ++fileIdCounter;
```

Aha! And here we have a case in point. Say the definition of `fileIdCounter` is something like the following:

```
int fileIdCounter = InitFileId();  // starts count at 100
```

If the compiler happens to initialize `fileIdCounter` before it initializes any `AAssert<T>::localFileId`, well and good—`localFileId` will get the expected value. Otherwise, the value set will be based on `fileIDCounter`'s pre-initialization value—namely, 0 for builtin types, and `localFileId` will end up with a value of 100 less than expected.

```
    if( !p.Invariant() )
    {
      cerr << "Invariant failed: file " << localFileId
           << ", " << typeid(p).name()
           << " at " << static_cast<void*>(&p) << endl;
      assert( false );
    }
}

template<class T>
class AInvariant
{
public:
  AInvariant( T& p ) : p_(p) { AAssert( p_ ); }
  ~AInvariant()              { AAssert( p_ ); }
private:
  T& p_;
};
#define AINVARIANT_GUARD AInvariant<AIType> invariantChecker( *this )
```

These helpers are an interesting idea in which any client class that would like to automatically check its class invariants before and after function calls simply writes a `typedef` of `AIType` to itself, then writes `AINVARIANT_GUARD;` as the first line of member functions. Not entirely bad, in itself.

In the client code below, these ideas unfortunately go astray. The main reason is that `AInvariant` hides calls to `assert()`, which will be automatically removed by the compiler when the program is built in non-debug mode. The following client code was likely written by a programmer who wasn't aware of this build dependency and the resulting change in side effects.

```
//----------------------------------------------------------------
template<class T>
class Array : private ArrayBase, public Container
{
  typedef Array AIType;
public:
  Array( size_t startingSize = 10 )
  : Container( startingSize ),
    ArrayBase( Container::GetType() ),
```

This constructor's initializer list has two potential errors. This first one is not necessarily an error, but was left in as a bit of a red herring.

1. If `GetType()` is a static member function, or a member function that does not use its `this` pointer (that is, uses no member data) and does not rely on any side effects of construction (for example, static usage counts), then this is merely poor style, but it will run correctly.

2. Otherwise (mainly, if `GetType()` is a normal nonstatic member function), we have a problem. Nonvirtual base classes are initialized in left-to-right order as they are declared, so `ArrayBase` is initialized before `Container`. Unfortunately, that means we're trying to use a member of the not-yet-initialized `Container` base subobject.

> **Guideline**
>
> *Always list base classes in a constructor's initialization list in the same order in which they appear in the class definition.*

```
used_(0),
size_(startingSize),
buffer_(new T[ size_ ])
```

This is a serious error, because the variables will actually be initialized in the order in which they appear later in the class definition:

```
buffer_(new T[ size_ ])
used_(0),
size_(startingSize),
```

Writing it this way makes the error obvious. The call to `new[]` will make buffer an unpredictable size—typically zero or something extremely large, depending on whether the compiler happens to initialize object memory to nulls before invoking constructors. At any rate, the initial allocation is unlikely to end up actually being for `startingSize` bytes.

> **Guideline**
>
> *Always list the data members in a constructor's initialization list in the same order in which they appear in the class definition.*

```
{
  AINVARIANT_GUARD;
}
```

We have a minor efficiency issue: The `Invariant()` function will be needlessly called twice, once during construction and again during destruction of the hidden temporary. This is a nit, though, and is unlikely to be a real issue.

```
void Resize( size_t newSize )
{
  AINVARIANT_GUARD;
  T* oldBuffer = buffer_;
  buffer_ = new T[newSize];
  copy( oldBuffer, oldBuffer+min(size_,newSize), buffer_ );
  delete[] oldBuffer;
  size_ = newSize;
}
```

There is a control flow problem here. Before reading on, examine the function again to see if you can spot a (hint: pretty obvious) control flow problem.

The answer is: This function is not exception-safe. If the call to `new[]` throws a `bad_alloc` exception, nothing bad happens; there's no leak in this particular case. However, if a `T` copy assignment operator throws an exception (in the course of the `copy()` operation), then not only is the current object left in an invalid state, but the original buffer is leaked, because all pointers to it are lost and so it can never be deleted.

The point of this function was to show that few, if any, programmers yet write exception-safe code as a matter of habit.

> **Guideline**
>
> *Always endeavor to write exception-safe code. Always structure code so that resources are correctly freed and data is in a consistent state even in the presence of exceptions.*

```
string PrintSizes()
{
  AINVARIANT_GUARD;
  char buf[30];
  return string("size = ") + itoa(size_,buf,10) +
         ", used = " + itoa(used_,buf,10) ;
}
```

The prototyped `itoa()` function uses the passed buffer as a scratch area. However, there's a control flow problem. There's no way to predict the order in which the expressions in the last line are evaluated, because the order in which function parameters are ordered is undefined and implementation-dependent.

What the last line really amounts to is something like this, since `operator+()` calls are still performed left-to-right:

```
return
  operator+(
    operator+(
      operator+( string("size = "),
                 itoa(size_,buf,10) ) ,
      ", used = " ) ,
    itoa(used_,buf,10) );
```

Say that `size_` is 10 and `used_` is 5. Then, if the outer `operator+()`'s first parameter is evaluated first, the output will be the correct "size = 10, used = 5" because the results of the first `itoa()` is used and stored in a temporary string before the second `itoa()` reuses the same buffer. If the outer `operator+()`'s second parameter is evaluated first (as it is on certain popular compilers), the output will be the incorrect "size = 10, used = 10" because the outer `itoa()` is executed first, then the inner `itoa()` will clobber the results of the outer `itoa()` before either value is used.

Common Mistake

Never write code that depends on the order of evaluation of function arguments.

```
bool Invariant()
{
  if( used_ > 0.9*size_ ) Resize( 2*size_ ) ;
  return used_ <= size_;
}
```

The call to Resize() has two problems.

1. In this case, the program wouldn't work at all anyway, because if the condition is true, then Resize() will be called, only to immediately call Invariant() again, which will find the condition still true and will call Resize() again, which—well, you get the idea.

2. What if, for efficiency, the writer of AAssert() decided to remove the error reporting and simply wrote "assert(p->Invariant());"? Then this client code becomes deplorable style, because it puts code with side effects inside an assert() call. This means the program's behavior will be different when compiled in debug mode than it is when compiled in release mode. Even without the first problem, this would be bad because it means that Array objects will resize at different times ,depending on the build mode. That will make the testers' lives a torture as they try to reproduce customer problems on a debug build that ends up having a different run-time memory image characteristics.

The bottom line is: Never write code with side effects inside a call to assert() (or something that might be one), and always make sure your recursions really terminate.

```
private:
  T*      buffer_;
  size_t used_, size_;
};

int f( int& x, int y = x ) { return x += y; }
```

The second parameter default isn't legal C++ at any rate, so this shouldn't compile under a conforming compiler (though some systems will take it). For the rest of this discussion, assume that the default value for y is 1.

```
int g( int& x )             { return x /= 2; }

int main( int, char*[] )
{
  int i = 42;
  cout << "f(" << i << ") = " << f(i) << ", "
       << "g(" << i << ") = " << g(i) << endl;
```

Here we run into parameter evaluation ordering again. Since there's no telling the order in which `f(i)` or `g(i)` will be executed (or, for that matter, the ordering of the two bald evaluations of `i` itself), the printed results can be quite incorrect. One example result is MSVC's "f(22) = 22, g(21) = 21", which means the compiler is likely evaluating all function arguments in order from right to left.

But isn't the result wrong? No, the compiler is right—and another compiler could print out something else and still be right, too, because the programmer is relying on something that is undefined in C++.

Common Mistake

Never write code that depends on the order of evaluation of function arguments.

```
    Array<char> a(20);
    cout << a.PrintSizes() << endl;
}
```

This should, of course, print "size = 20, used = 0", but because of the already-discussed bug in `PrintSizes()`, some popular compilers print "size = 20, used = 20", which is clearly incorrect.

Perhaps Dorothy wasn't quite right after all about her menagerie of animals—the following might be closer:

"Parameters and globals and exceptions, oh my!"
—Dorothy, after an intermediate C++ course

Afterword

If you've enjoyed the puzzles and problems in this book, then I have good news for you. This is not the end, for *Guru of the Week #30* was not the last *GotW,* nor have I stopped writing articles in various programming magazines.

Today, on the Internet, new *GotW* issues are being published and discussed and debated regularly on the newsgroup *comp.lang.c++.moderated*, and are archived at the official *GotW* Website at *www.gotw.ca*. As I write this, in June 1999, we're already up to #55. To give you a taste for what's coming, a small sampling of the new *GotW* issues includes fresh material on such topics as the following:

- More information on popular themes, including the safe use of `auto_ptr`, namespaces, and exception-safety issues and techniques, taking the next step beyond Items 8 through 17, 31 through 34, and 37.
- A three-part series on reference-counting and copy-on-write techniques, including unusual performance implications in multithreaded (or multithread-capable) environments, with extensive test harness code and statistical measurements. There's material here that you usually don't see discussed anywhere else.
- Many puzzles about the safe and effective use of standard library, especially containers (like `vector` and `map`) and the standard streams. This includes more information about how to best extend the standard library, in the spirit of Items 2 and 3.
- A nifty game: writing a MasterMind-playing program in as few statements as possible.

And that's just a small sample. If there is enough interest in the book you're holding in your hands now, my intention is to produce another volume containing expanded and reorganized forms of the next batch of issues, again including the text of the other C++ engineering articles and columns that I'm writing for *C/C++ Users Journal*, and other magazines.

I hope you've enjoyed the book, and that you'll continue to let me know what interesting topics you'd like to see covered in the future; see the Website mentioned earlier for how to submit requests. Some topics you've read about herein were prompted by e-mails like these.

Thanks again to all who have expressed interest and support for *GotW* and this book. I hope you've found this material to be useful in your daily work, as you keep on writing faster, cleaner, and safer C++ programs.

Bibliography

Barton94: John Barton and Lee Nackman, *Scientific and Engineering C++*. Addison-Wesley, 1994.

Cargill92: Tom Cargill, *C++ Programming Style*. Addison-Wesley, 1992.

Cargill94: Tom Cargill, "Exception Handling: A False Sense of Security." *C++ Report*, 9(6), Nov.–Dec. 1994.

Cline95: Marshall Cline and Greg Lomow, *C++ FAQs*. Addison-Wesley, 1995.

Cline99: Marshall Cline, Greg Lomow, and Mike Girou, *C++ FAQs, Second Edition*. Addison Wesley Longman, 1999.

Coplien92: James Coplien. *Advanced C++ Programming Styles and Idioms*. Addison-Wesley, 1992.

Ellis90: Margaret Ellis and Bjarne Stroustrup, *The Annotated C++ Reference Manual*. Addison-Wesley, 1990.

Gamma95: Erich Gamma, Richard Helm, Ralph Johnson, and John Vlissides, *Design Patterns: Elements of Reusable Object-Oriented Software*. Addison-Wesley, 1995.

Keffer95: Thomas Keffer, *Rogue Wave C++ Design, Implementation, and Style Guide*. Rogue Wave Software, 1995.

Koenig97: Andrew Koenig and Barbara Moo, *Ruminations on C++*. Addison Wesley Longman, 1997.

Lakos96: John Lakos, *Large-Scale C++ Software Design*. Addison-Wesley, 1996.

Lippman97: Stan Lippman (ed.), *C++ Gems*. SIGS / Cambridge University Press, 1997.

Lippman98: Stan Lippman and Josée Lajoie, *C++ Primer, Third Edition*. Addison Wesley Longman, 1998.

Martin95: Robert C. Martin, *Designing Object-Oriented Applications Using the Booch Method*. Prentice-Hall, 1995.

Martin00: Robert C. Martin (ed.), *C++ Gems II*. SIGS / Cambridge University Press, 2000.

Meyers96: Scott Meyers, *More Effective C++*. Addison-Wesley, 1996.

Meyers98: Scott Meyers, *Effective C++, Second Edition*. Addison Wesley Longman, 1998.

Meyers99: Scott Meyers, *Effective C++ CD*. Addison Wesley Longman, 1999. (See also http://www.gotw.ca/publications/xc++/sm_effective.htm)

Murray93: Robert Murray, *C++ Strategies and Tactics*. Addison-Wesley, 1993.

Myers97: Nathan Myers, "The Empty Base C++ Optimization." *Dr. Dobb's Journal,* Aug. 1997.

Stroustrup94: Bjarne Stroustrup, *The Design and Evolution of C++*. Addison-Wesley, 1994.

Stroustrup97: Bjarne Stroustrup, *The C++ Progamming Language, Third Edition*. Addison Wesley Longman, 1997.

Sutter98: Herb Sutter, "C++ State of the Union." *C++ Report,* 10(1), Jan. 1998.

Sutter98(a): Herb Sutter, "Uses and Abuses of Inheritance, Part 1." *C++ Report,* 10(9), Oct. 1998.

Sutter99: Herb Sutter, "Uses and Abuses of Inheritance, Part 2." *C++ Report,* 11(1), Jan. 1999.

Index

J

K

L

M

T

U